Previously published:

Maths and Calculator skills for Science Students		March 2016
·	Maths (The Chemistry bits) for GCSE Science	May 2016
·	Science revision Guide	April 2017
·	Maths Revision Guide	April 2017
·	Summer Start for A-Level Chemistry	May 2017
·	Atoms, Electrons, Structure and Bonding Workbook	June 2017
·	GCSE Maths Grade 7, 8 and 9 Revision Questions	September 2017
·	75 long answer questions for GCSE science	April 2018
·	Stepping Further; a comprehensive guide to applying to university	July 2018
·	Organic Chemistry Notebook	August 2018
·	AQA GCSE Combined Science Required Practicals Exam Practice Workbook	February 2019
·	AQA GCSE Biology Required Practicals Exam Practice Workbook	February 2019
·	AQA GCSE Chemistry Required Practicals Exam Practice Workbook	February 2019
·	AQA GCSE Physics Required Practicals Exam Practice Workbook	February 2019

Coming soon...

- Complete Maths workbook
- Organic Chemistry Workbook
- Maths for A-Level Chemistry
- Maths (The Physics bits) for GCSE Combined Science
- Maths (The Physics bits) for GCSE Triple Science
- Summer Start for A-Level Physics
- Summer Start for A-Level Biology

Chances are if you want a maths/science book I've written it or I am writing it.

For full book listings, visit www.PrimroseKitten.com and follow @primrose_kitten

GCSE Geography Complete Workbook for Eduqas B

Contents

Revision Workbook

Revision techniques..**8**

Different techniques **8**

Revision timetable **10**
Planning Tips for your timetable 10
Weekdays...11
Weekend...12

The Exam..**14**

Exam command words **14**

Examples **15**

Tips in the exam **17**

Speak like a Geographer: **17**

Exam dates 2019 ....**18**

Theme 1: CHANGING PLACES - CHANGING ECONOMIES.....................**19**

Key Idea 1.1: Urbanisation in contrasting global cities **19**
Knowledge Checklist 19
Practice questions 20

Key Idea 1.2: Urban and rural processes and change in the UK **26**
Knowledge Checklist 26
Practice questions 28

Key Idea 1.3: A global perspective on development issues **34**
Knowledge Checklist 34
Practice questions 36

Theme 2: CHANGING ENVIRONMENTS...**42**

Key Idea 2.1: Shaping the landscape - coasts and coastal management..**42**
Knowledge Checklist 42
Practice questions 43

Key Idea 2.2: Shaping the landscape - rivers and river management
....**48**

Knowledge Checklist 48
Practice questions 50

Key Idea 2.3: Weather and climate **57**
Knowledge Checklist 57
Practice questions 59

Key Idea 2.4: Climate change - cause and effect **64**
Knowledge Checklist 64
Practice questions 65

Theme 3: ENVIRONMENTAL CHALLENGES **70**

Key Idea 3.1: How ecosystems function & Key Idea 3.2: Ecosystems under threat **70**
Knowledge Checklist 70
Practice questions 71

Key Idea 3.3: Water resources and management **77**
Knowledge Checklist 77
Practice questions 78

Key Idea 3.4: Desertification **81**
Knowledge Checklist 81
Practice questions 82

Case Study Booklet

Case studies – An Introduction **87**

Case Study Questions **88**

Examples of Case Study Questions **88**

How to answer a case study **89**

What you need to know for the exam? **90**

Structuring your answer **91**

Structure Strips **91**

P.E.E.L **92**

Examples **93**

Short level questions **93**
Example 1 93
Comments on Example 1: 94
Example 2 95
Comments on Example 2: 95
Example 3: 96
Comments on Example 3: 97

Extended question **98**
  Example 4: 98
  Comments on Example 4: 100

Exam board specifications **101**

Eduqas B **101**
  Knowledge checklist...101
  Mark scheme...102

1. Case Studies - Weather **103**

  1.1 - Hurricane Katrina, August 2005... **103**

  1.2 - Typhoon Haiyan, November 2013. .... **104**

  1.3 - Storm Desmond, December 2015 .... **105**

  1.4 - Attica Wildfires, July 2018 .... **106**

  1.5 - Great Australia Drought, 2002-2009................................. **107**

2. Case Studies – Ecosystems **108**

  2.1 - Amazon Rainforest, multiple examples **108**

  2.2 – Greenland **110**

3. Case Studies - Tectonics **111**

  3.1 - La-Aquila Earthquake, April 2009 .... **111**

  3.2 - Bam Earthquake, December 2003 .... **112**

  3.3 – Eyjafjallajökull volcano, March 2010 .... **113**

  3.4 - Soufriere Hills volcano, 1995-1997 .... **114**

4. Case Studies - Rivers **115**

  4.1 - Boscastle flood, August 2004.. **115**

  4.2 - Somerset Levels floods, winter 2013-2014.......................... **116**

  4.3 - Management of the River Severn at Shrewsbury **118**

  4.4 - Landforms on the River Tees **119**

5. Case Studies - Coasts **120**

  5.1 - Storm Surge, December 2013 .... **120**

  5.2 - Landforms on the Holderness Coastline.............................. **121**

  5.3 - Landforms on the Dorset Coastline **122**

5.4 - Managed Realignment - Medmerry scheme............................ 123

5.5 - Shoreline Management Plan - Borth.................................... 124

5.6 - Thames Gateway scheme.. 125

5.7 - Coastlines vulnerable to rising sea levels in the UK 126

5.8 - Coastlines vulnerable to rising sea levels - Maldives........... 127

6. Case Studies - Urbanisation...128

6.1 – Urbanisation in Mumbai 128

6.2 – Urbanisation in London 129

6.3 - Urbanisation in Leeds 131

7. Case Studies - Development / Global issues..............................133

7.1 - Mali 133

7.2 - Nike as MNC case study 134

7.3 - Aid projects 135

Fieldwork booklet

Key information..137

Geographical and numerical Skills 137

Fieldwork element:... 137

Fieldwork Tips... 138

What you will need to remember:..138

How to: Analysis the results 139

Graphical 139

Maps..139

Photographs 140

Examples 140

Geographical and Numerical Skills 144

Knowledge Checklist...144

Practice Questions..146

Fieldwork 149

Knowledge Checklist...149

Your HUMAN fieldwork... 150

Practice Questions..152

Your PHYSICAL fieldwork.. 156

Practice Questions..158

Unseen fieldwork example #1 ....**162**
    Practice exam-style questions: 162

Specific topic fieldwork questions **171**

Coastal 171

River 172

Urban environment 173

Rural environment 175

Unseen fieldwork example #2 ....**176**

Model Fieldwork Summary **184**

Answers

Exam command words: 189

Revision workbook answers 190

THEME 1: CHANGING PLACES – CHANGING ECONOMIES 190
    KEY IDEA 1.1: Urbanization in contrasting global cities 190
    KEY IDEA: 1.2 Urban and rural processes and change in the UK 192
    KEY IDEA: 1.3 A global perspective on development issues...194

THEME 2: CHANGING ENVIRONMENTS 196
    KEY IDEA 2.1: Shaping the landscape - coasts and coastal management...196
    KEY IDEA: 2.2 Shaping the landscape – rivers and river management 199
    KEY IDEA: 2.3 Weather and Climate...202
    KEY IDEA: 2.4: Climate change - cause and effect...205

THEME 3: ENVIRONMENTAL CHALLENGES 207
    KEY IDEA: 3.1: How ecosystems function and 3.2 Ecosystems under threat...207
    KEY IDEA 3.2 Water Resources and Management 209
    KEY IDEA 3.3: Desertification 210

Fieldwork booklet answers **212**

Geographical and Numeracy Skills Answers 212

Your Human fieldwork 214

Your Physical fieldwork 216

Unseen fieldwork example 1 217

Specific topic fieldwork questions 221
    Coastal...221
    Urban environment...222
    Rural environment...223

Unseen Fieldwork Example 223

Appendix 227

    Revision Timetable.. 228

    Revision Planner 235

    Revision Tracker 236

Revision Workbook

Revision techniques

Revision is the key to success, but adopting a variety of revision methods is best.

Here is a list of some of the better general methods:

- Create your own glossary, including command words
- Create flash cards of case studies / processes / topics / themes
- Use post-it notes to contain small facts
- Create case study poster – keep the information to the point / condensed.
- Organise revision notes into themes / topics.

Different techniques

1. Active Revision

- Say it out load
- Walk around whilst revising
- Use fragrances for different topics

2. Bodily Revision

- Using your own body helps to sharpen the memory!
- For example:

    - Image water consumption on the top of your head
    - Image wealth in HIC is in your mouth
    - Image industry use is your arms

3. Colour my Revision – very easy!

- Chose 5 to 10 different colours and make a clear key.
- Work through a topic / idea and then try to explain how each point fits into a colour / category.
- For example:

    - RED: effect of the process on people
    - BLUE: how the process happens e.g. step by step
    - GREEN: effects of an event on the environment

4. AMGIAM – acronyms and mnemonics great in aiding memory

- Acronym is an abbreviation formed from the initial words
- For example:

  - Multi National Corporation is **MNC**
  - Demographical Transition Model is **DTM**

- Mnemonics refer to a sentence in which the initial letters of each words provide an aid to remember especially something in a particular order or process.

5. Cause, Event and Effects

- Create a flow diagram – very handy on case studies:

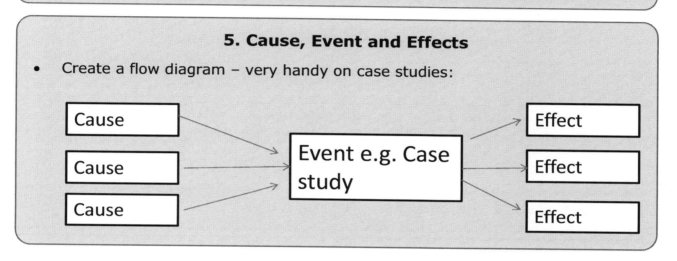

6. Teach it! (my personal fav!)

- This when you share the love for Geography with your family and friends!
- Create it in stages:

  - *Multiple choice, Gap fill exercise, Diagrams with missing labels*
  - *Reading and comprehension tasks and many more*

- Then get your person to complete and mark it!

Revision timetable

Planning Tips for your timetable

1. Write your timetable in pencil (or make a version on the computer) so you can change things around if necessary.

2. Start by thinking about what activities you can't miss (dinner, clubs or TV programs) and put these into your timetable.

3. Plan in when you need to do your homework to get it in on time.

4. On top of your homework time, aim for a minimum of 2 extra hours on a weekday and 4 hours each day over the weekend.

5. Plan to revise for 1 hour per subject each week (this is in addition to homework) fill in the table below to help you work out how much time you need to spend on revision.

Subject	Group	Priority	Number of hours per week
Maths	Core	High (+2 hours)	
English literature	Core	High (+2 hours)	
English language	Core	High (+2 hours)	
	A level choice	High (+2 hours)	
	A level choice	High (+2 hours)	
	A level choice	High (+2 hours)	
	A level choice	High (+2 hours)	
	Subjects I struggle with	Medium (+1 hour)	
	Subjects I struggle with	Medium (+1 hour)	
	Subjects I struggle with	Medium (+1 hour)	
	Subjects I struggle with	Medium (+1 hour)	

6. Fill in the timetable spreading out the subjects (e.g., don't do a whole day of Maths, do a bit each day) put contrasting subjects next to each other, to give your brain a break (e.g. English and Physics).

7. Stick to the timetable, it will help ensure you cover each subject and spread out your revision.

Weekdays

Monday	
Time	Revision Subject/Topics
	Homework
5-minute break	
5-minute break	
5-minute break	

*See appendix for a whole week revision timetable, revision planner and revision tracker

Weekend

Saturday		Sunday	
Time	Revision Subject/Topics	Time	Revision Subject/Topics
5-minute break			
5-minute break			
5-minute break			
5-minute break			

5-minute break			
5-minute break			

The Exam

Exam command words

It is really important to look at the command words of questions. These words tell you how to answer the question. Here are the main words:

Describe	Say what it looks like e.g. the classroom is painted white.
Explain	Say why it is like this e.g. the Head teacher decided all classrooms will be painted white.
Evaluate	The Head teacher did a questionnaire and using the results saw
Analyse	The results showed that 90% of pupils didn't notice the colour.
Assess...	Look at the impact / effect / causes and come to a conclusion. Consider multiple points

Make sure you understand the difference between these command words. This is often where people miss out on easy marks:

- annotate and label...

- describe and explain...

- effects and impacts...

Read carefully when it says:
- Use the material given...
- Using the data provided...
- Looking at the area 248782 of map X...
- Using a case study / example...

Highlight these parts of a question and ensure that you include at least twice in your answer.

Examples

1. Look at the example below without the command word, do you know how they want to you to answer the question?

.... the impact on the environment.

If you put the following words at the start of the question, the answers are very different.

Describe   Explain   Analysis   Evaluate

Look at the following examples and put the correct command word into the box.

1		The decrease of vegetation has resulted in desertification and further damage.
2		The variety of plants has decreased.
3		The decrease of plants is over 50%.
4		With the decreased vegetation, biodiversity has decreased.

2. Look at the two examples below, what do you think makes the stronger answer better?

Discuss the impacts of a flood on the people and the environment

Boscastle was an example of a flash flood. It was caused by large volume of water and having a short river catchment and narrow channels. No one died because of the good rescue work done by the emergency services. However, the houses and businesses were destroyed so people will have been forced to move. The environment was also damaged with mudflows in the area.

Discuss the impacts of a flood on the people and the environment

Boscastle was an example of a flash flood (August 2004). It was caused by large volume of water and having a short river catchment and narrow channels where it has August rainfall in just 3 hours. No one died because of the good rescue work done by the emergency services - 120 people rescued by 7 helicopters which will have cost money. However, the houses and businesses were destroyed so people will have been forced to move – it took 9 months to rebuild, cost £15million and insurance companies had a high bill, it could make it difficult to insure in the future. The environment was also damaged with mudflows in the area. Trees were uprooted and this impacts future floods because soil is loose as well trees help intercept rainfall and delay the lag time which could increase the risk of flooding in the future. Farmland would also have been damaged which will have impacts on crop yields.

Tips in the exam

- Highlight the key command word.
- Put alternative words above any words that you struggle with.
- Look at the mark – if it is a 4 plus mark you need depth e.g. examples, development of points.

Speak like a Geographer:

- It is so important in the exam that you use not only correct terminology but also to answer with depth.
- Consider the following:

- Describe the location...

    Do not just say "Africa has a hot climate". Instead use terms and phrases such as:

    - *The horn of Africa*
    - *The North West of Africa*
    - *The region of...*
    - *South of the tropic of cancer*

- Talking about a case study

    Do not use "it is a poor country" or "it is a hot country". Instead use terms and phrases such as:

    - *The GDP of the country suggests*
    - *The climate is mainly ……. in the summer.*

- Talking of impacts

    Don't use sentences like "it means more people have money" or "lots of homes were flooded". Instead use terms and phrases such as:

    - *The average income of families increased by 25% except for the lower income, whereby their incomes stayed the same.*
    - *More than 600 homes were flooding, resulting in over 800 people made homeless.*

Exam dates 2019

Dates might be changed, so make sure to double check.

Date	Exam	Units covered
21st May PM 2019	**Investigating Geographical Issues** Written examination: 1 hour 45 minutes 40% of qualification 96 marks (plus 4 marks for spelling, punctuation, grammar and use of specialist terms) Three structured questions, each of 32 marks, will include opportunities for assessment using multiple choice, data response, short open response and extended responses. At least one open response question will synthesize knowledge and understanding of the UK as a whole.	All
5th June PM 2019	**Problem Solving Geography** Written examination: 1 hour 30 minutes 30% of qualification 72 marks (plus 4 marks for spelling, punctuation, grammar and use of specialist terms)	Can be from any section of the course.
13th June AM 2019	**Component 3 - Applied Fieldwork Enquiry** Written examination: 1 hour 30 minutes 30% of qualification 72 marks (plus 4 marks for spelling, punctuation, grammar and use of specialist terms) Component 3 is a written examination in three parts Part A will assess approaches to fieldwork methodology, representation and analysis. Part B will assess how fieldwork enquiry may be used to investigate geography's conceptual frameworks. Part C will assess the application of broad geographical concepts to a wider UK context and assess the ability to make and justify a decision.	Fieldwork and UK

Theme 1: CHANGING PLACES - CHANGING ECONOMIES

Key Idea 1.1: Urbanisation in contrasting global cities

Knowledge Checklist

Specification statement These are the bits the exam board wants you to know, make sure you can do all of these…	Self-assessment		
	First review 4-7 months before exam	Second review 1-2 months before exam	Final review Week before exam
I can describe the processes of urbanization and re-urbanization and explain the differences between them.	☺ ☺ ☹	☺ ☺ ☹	☺ ☺ ☹
I can give the meaning of global city and megacity and explain the differences between them.	☺ ☺ ☹	☺ ☺ ☹	☺ ☺ ☹
I can describe the location of global cities	☺ ☺ ☹	☺ ☺ ☹	☺ ☺ ☹
I can describe the development of global cities over time	☺ ☺ ☹	☺ ☺ ☹	☺ ☺ ☹
I can describe the distribution of global cities	☺ ☺ ☹	☺ ☺ ☹	☺ ☺ ☹
I can give the reasons for the growth of the urban area you have studied and Mumbai including natural population and migration.	☺ ☺ ☹	☺ ☺ ☹	☺ ☺ ☹
I can give push factors and pull factors for both cities.	☺ ☺ ☹	☺ ☺ ☹	☺ ☺ ☹
I can say where people are moving to this city from e.g. rural areas, other parts of the country.	☺ ☺ ☹	☺ ☺ ☹	☺ ☺ ☹
I can describe social, economic and cultural patterns in your locations. E.g. where do rich people live, where do ethnic groups live.	☺ ☺ ☹	☺ ☺ ☹	☺ ☺ ☹
I can describe the problems in your locations have with poverty and deprivation e.g. food banks, crime, homelessness	☺ ☺ ☹	☺ ☺ ☹	☺ ☺ ☹

I can describe the problems in your locations have with housing e.g. slums and housing shortages	☺ ☺ ☹	☺ ☺ ☹	☺ ☺ ☹
I can describe the problems your locations have with infrastructure (roads), transport and waste disposal	☺ ☺ ☹	☺ ☺ ☹	☺ ☺ ☹
I can give examples of strategies which aim to reduce inequality and improve the lives of people living in Mumbai e.g. self-help schemes, slum clearance programmes, housing projects and mass transit schemes	☺ ☺ ☹	☺ ☺ ☹	☺ ☺ ☹
I can give examples of strategies which aim to reduce inequality and improve the lives of people living in your urban area e.g. sustainable homes and communities	☺ ☺ ☹	☺ ☺ ☹	☺ ☺ ☹

Practice questions

1. Define the following terms:

   a) global city and megacity

   ....
   ....
   ....
   ....

   (2 marks)

   b) Explain the differences between them.

   ....
   ....
   ....
   ....
   ....
   ....
   ....
   ....

   (4 marks)

2. Describe the distribution of global cities around the world and the link between them and mega cities.

....
....
....
....
....
....
....
....

(4 marks)

3. Explain the main reasons for growth within urban areas in HICs.

....
....
....
....
....
....
....
....
....
....
....
....
....
....
....
....

(6 marks)

4. Explain the main reasons for the growth within urban areas in developing countries.

....
....
....
....
....
....
....
....
....
....
....
....
....
....
....
....
....

(6 marks)

5. Using your chosen location, describe the social, economic and cultural patterns within the area.

....
....
....
....
....
....
....
....
....
....
....

(4 marks)

6. Describe how urban developments have changed in the UK over time.

....
....
....
....
....
....
....
....
....
....
....

(4 marks)

7. Give 3 impacts of urbanisation on both your locations.

....
....
....
....
....
....
....
....
....
....
....

(6 marks)

8. Explain the problems in your locations have with poverty and deprivation.

....
....
....
....
....
....
....
....
....
....
....
....
....
....
....
....
....

(6 marks)

9. Explain how infrastructure (roads), transport and waste disposal have impacts on your urban area and how it is being resolved.

....
....
....
....
....
....
....
....
....
....
....
....
....
....
....
....
....
....

(6 marks)

10. Analyse the strategies which aim to reduce inequality and improve the lives of people living within developing urban areas.

....
....
....
....
....
....
....
....
....
....
....
....
....
....
....
....
....
....
....
....
....
....
....
....

(8 marks)

Key Idea 1.2: Urban and rural processes and change in the UK

Knowledge Checklist

Specification statement These are the bits the exam board wants you to know, make sure you can do all of these…	Self-assessment		
	First review 4-7 months before exam	Second review 1-2 months before exam	Final review Week before exam
I can describe the processes of urbanization, suburbanization and re-urbanization. I can identify key differences between them.	☺ ☺ ☹	☺ ☺ ☹	☺ ☺ ☹
I can give the definition of counter-urbanization, community, greenfield and brownfield.	☺ ☺ ☹	☺ ☺ ☹	☺ ☺ ☹
I can give two examples of ways that rural areas in the UK are changing.	☺ ☺ ☹	☺ ☺ ☹	☺ ☺ ☹
I can describe at least three different zones in UK cities and name distinctive features.	☺ ☺ ☹	☺ ☺ ☹	☺ ☺ ☹
I can give the meaning of key retail terms – range, threshold population and catchment area.	☺ ☺ ☹	☺ ☺ ☹	☺ ☺ ☹
I understand the main features of high street and out-of-town retail locations.	☺ ☺ ☹	☺ ☺ ☹	☺ ☺ ☹
I can describe how leisure use can damage the environment.	☺ ☺ ☹	☺ ☺ ☹	☺ ☺ ☹
I can explain why people commute and use examples.	☺ ☺ ☹	☺ ☺ ☹	☺ ☺ ☹
I can give at least three reasons why some people move from cities to the countryside.	☺ ☺ ☹	☺ ☺ ☹	☺ ☺ ☹
I can name one region that has a housing shortage and explain why this has happened.	☺ ☺ ☹	☺ ☺ ☹	☺ ☺ ☹
I can give two reasons why some people leave rural areas of the UK.	☺ ☺ ☹	☺ ☺ ☹	☺ ☺ ☹

I can give two reasons why retailing in some high streets is in decline.	☺ ☺ ☹	☺ ☺ ☹	☺ ☺ ☹
I can define the following – high street, out of town shopping, mobile shopping and internet shopping.	☺ ☺ ☹	☺ ☺ ☹	☺ ☺ ☹
I can describe and explain the processes of urban change to suggest why towns/cities have different and distinctive zones (like areas that need regeneration).	☺ ☺ ☹	☺ ☺ ☹	☺ ☺ ☹
I can identify the issues that arise from population change in at least one urban and one rural area of the UK.	☺ ☺ ☹	☺ ☺ ☹	☺ ☺ ☹
I can evaluate the advantages and disadvantages of building on greenfield sites.	☺ ☺ ☹	☺ ☺ ☹	☺ ☺ ☹
I can evaluate the advantages and disadvantages of building on brownfield sites.	☺ ☺ ☹	☺ ☺ ☹	☺ ☺ ☹
I can explain why different groups of people have different points of view about how to make urban or rural communities sustainable.	☺ ☺ ☹	☺ ☺ ☹	☺ ☺ ☹
I can define the term honeypot and give examples of issues within these areas.	☺ ☺ ☹	☺ ☺ ☹	☺ ☺ ☹
I can give the advantages and disadvantages of leisure use on a rural honeypot.	☺ ☺ ☹	☺ ☺ ☹	☺ ☺ ☹
I can evaluate the positive and negative impacts of major sporting events.	☺ ☺ ☹	☺ ☺ ☹	☺ ☺ ☹
I can demonstrate how sustainable communities might be effective with use of at least one method.	☺ ☺ ☹	☺ ☺ ☹	☺ ☺ ☹
I can identify recent changes in retailing and show that I can connect the causes and effects of change.	☺ ☺ ☹	☺ ☺ ☹	☺ ☺ ☹
I can rank the effectiveness of strategies to manage a place that is under pressure from too many visitors.	☺ ☺ ☹	☺ ☺ ☹	☺ ☺ ☹

Practice questions

1. Define the following terms:

    a) Counter-urbanisation

    ....
    ....

    b) Brownfield

    ....
    ....

    c) Greenfield

    ....
    ....

    (3 marks)

2. Explain the advantages and disadvantages of redevelopment and development
    has on both greenfield and brownfield sites.

    ....
    ....
    ....
    ....
    ....
    ....
    ....
    ....
    ....
    ....
    ....
    ....
    ....
    ....
    ....
    ....

    (6 marks)

3. Using London as an example, explain why it has a housing shortage and the impacts this has.

....
....
....
....
....
....
....
....
....
....
....
....
....
....
....
....
....

(6 marks)

4. Describe how rural areas in the UK are changing.

....
....
....
....
....
....
....
....
....
....
....

(4 marks)

5. Give main features of high street and out-of-town retail locations and explain at least two of them.

....
....
....
....
....
....
....
....
....
....
....
....
....
....
....
....
....
....

(6 marks)

6. Define the following terms and explain how this is changing retail.

   a) high street

....
....
....
....
....
....
....

   b) out of town shopping

....
....
....
....
....
....
....

c) mobile shopping

....
....
....
....
....
....
....

d) internet shopping

....
....
....
....
....
....
....

(8 marks)

7. Define the term honeypot and give examples of issues within these areas.

....
....
....
....
....
....
....
....
....
....
....
....
....

(4 marks)

8. Evaluate the effectiveness of strategies to manage a place that is under pressure from too many visitors.

....
....
....
....
....
....
....
....
....
....
....
....
....
....
....
....
....
....
....
....
....
....
....
....
....
....
....

(8 marks)

9. Create a table with the positive and negative impacts of major sporting event (e.g. Olympics, Tour de Yorkshire).

(4 marks)

Sporting event:	
Positive	Negative

10. Define the term sustainable community and using an example, explain how a sustainable community operates.

....

....

....

....

....

....

....

....

....

....

....

....

....

....

....

....

....

(6 marks)

Key Idea 1.3: A global perspective on development issues

Knowledge Checklist

Specification statement These are the bits the exam board wants you to know, make sure you can do all of these…	Self-assessment		
	First review 4-7 months before exam	Second review 1-2 months before exam	Final review Week before exam
I can define the terms: NIC, LIC, LEDC, MNC.	☺ ☺ ☹	☺ ☺ ☹	☺ ☺ ☹
I can describe three different indicators of development.	☺ ☺ ☹	☺ ☺ ☹	☺ ☺ ☹
I can describe how global patterns of development are uneven.	☺ ☺ ☹	☺ ☺ ☹	☺ ☺ ☹
I can define each of the trade terms: tariffs, trade blocs and 'fair' trade.	☺ ☺ ☹	☺ ☺ ☹	☺ ☺ ☹
I can give an example of a long-term development aid programme.	☺ ☺ ☹	☺ ☺ ☹	☺ ☺ ☹
I can explain why trade, technology, industry and migration help to create stronger links between countries.	☺ ☺ ☹	☺ ☺ ☹	☺ ☺ ☹
I can give reasons why MNCs locate in more than one country.	☺ ☺ ☹	☺ ☺ ☹	☺ ☺ ☹
I can give reasons for the emergence of NICs.	☺ ☺ ☹	☺ ☺ ☹	☺ ☺ ☹
I can identify the benefits and disadvantages of MNC investment on the environment, economy and society in one region/country.	☺ ☺ ☹	☺ ☺ ☹	☺ ☺ ☹
I can bring together data from different sources to build an argument.	☺ ☺ ☹	☺ ☺ ☹	☺ ☺ ☹
I can select appropriate data from a large data set to make comparisons between two countries at different levels of development.	☺ ☺ ☹	☺ ☺ ☹	☺ ☺ ☹

I can compare the advantages of a long-term development programme for both the donor and recipient country.	☺ ☺ ☹	☺ ☺ ☹	☺ ☺ ☹
I can identify where data is unreliable due to inaccuracies, or data gaps.	☺ ☺ ☹	☺ ☺ ☹	☺ ☺ ☹
I can explain the limitations of using only one type of data to describe patterns of global development.	☺ ☺ ☹	☺ ☺ ☹	☺ ☺ ☹
I can evaluate that global trade, industry and migration are drivers of change and development.	☺ ☺ ☹	☺ ☺ ☹	☺ ☺ ☹
I can evaluate the benefits of fair trade.	☺ ☺ ☹	☺ ☺ ☹	☺ ☺ ☹
I can evaluate the positive and negative consequences of development in one NIC.	☺ ☺ ☹	☺ ☺ ☹	☺ ☺ ☹
I can summarize the evidence that suggests that NICs are closing the development gap much more quickly than LICs.	☺ ☺ ☹	☺ ☺ ☹	☺ ☺ ☹
I can justify two criteria for measuring development issues in contrasting countries.	☺ ☺ ☹	☺ ☺ ☹	☺ ☺ ☹
I can decide whether MNC investment has been beneficial for one country I have studied. Justify my decision.	☺ ☺ ☹	☺ ☺ ☹	☺ ☺ ☹
I can define the following terms tariffs/ trade blocs/ quotas.	☺ ☺ ☹	☺ ☺ ☹	☺ ☺ ☹
I can explain how the structure of trade (e.g. tariffs/ trade blocs/ quotas etc.) impacts on patterns of global development. Draw conclusions.	☺ ☺ ☹	☺ ☺ ☹	☺ ☺ ☹
I can evaluate and justify the development priorities for one LIC or NIC where long-term development aid is needed.	☺ ☺ ☹	☺ ☺ ☹	☺ ☺ ☹

Practice questions

1. Describe three different indicators of development.

....
....
....
....
....
....
....
....
....
....
....

(3 marks)

2. Explain why trade, technology, industry and migration help to create stronger links between countries.

....
....
....
....
....
....
....
....
....
....
....
....
....
....
....

(4 marks)

3. Define the term: MNC and give two examples.

....
....
....
....
....

(3 marks)

4. Explain the reasons for the emergence of NICs.

....
....
....
....
....
....
....
....
....
....
....

(4 marks)

5. Explain the benefits and disadvantages of MNC investment on the environment, economy and society in one region/country.

....
....
....
....
....
....
....
....
....
....
....
....
....
....
....
....
....
....
....
....
....
....
....
....
....
....
....
....

(8 marks)

6. Define what fair trade is and explain the benefits.

....
....
....
....
....
....
....
....
....

(4 marks)

7. Explain the positive and negative consequences of development in one NIC.

....
....
....
....
....
....
....
....
....
....

(4 marks)

8. Define the following terms:

a) Tariffs

....
....

b) Trade blocs

....
....

c) Quotas.

....
....

(3 marks)

9. Explain how the structure of trade (e.g. tariffs/ trade blocs/ quotas etc) impacts on patterns of global development.

....
....
....
....
....
....
....
....
....
....
....

(4 marks)

10. Assess the development priorities for one NIC where long-term development aid is needed.

....

....

....

....

....

....

....

....

....

....

....

....

....

....

....

....

....

....

....

....

(8 marks)

Theme 2: CHANGING ENVIRONMENTS

Key Idea 2.1: Shaping the landscape - coasts and coastal management

Knowledge Checklist

Specification statement These are the bits the exam board wants you to know, make sure you can do all of these…	Self-assessment		
	First review 4-7 months before exam	Second review 1-2 months before exam	Final review Week before exam
I understand how tidal movement occurs.	☺ ☺ ☹	☺ ☺ ☹	☺ ☺ ☹
I understand the two main types of waves.	☺ ☺ ☹	☺ ☺ ☹	☺ ☺ ☹
I understand the different types of erosion.	☺ ☺ ☹	☺ ☺ ☹	☺ ☺ ☹
I can describe what mass movement is and share examples and impacts.	☺ ☺ ☹	☺ ☺ ☹	☺ ☺ ☹
I can explain how geology can affect coastal landscapes.	☺ ☺ ☹	☺ ☺ ☹	☺ ☺ ☹
I can explain how resistant rock formation are created and use examples.	☺ ☺ ☹	☺ ☺ ☹	☺ ☺ ☹
I am able to define and explain the process of longshore drift.	☺ ☺ ☹	☺ ☺ ☹	☺ ☺ ☹
I can explain what a groin is and am able to explain how it prevents longshore drift	☺ ☺ ☹	☺ ☺ ☹	☺ ☺ ☹
I can describe and explain the processes of transportation occurs, including traction, saltation, suspension and solution / LSD.	☺ ☺ ☹	☺ ☺ ☹	☺ ☺ ☹
I can describe and explain how deposition creates features (spit and bar, estuaries) are formed.	☺ ☺ ☹	☺ ☺ ☹	☺ ☺ ☹
I understand how seasonal weather and extreme events effect the coastline	☺ ☺ ☹	☺ ☺ ☹	☺ ☺ ☹

I can describe the different methods of soft engineering and how effective they are.	☺ ☺ ☹	☺ ☺ ☹	☺ ☺ ☹
I can describe and explain different methods of hard engineering and their effectiveness.	☺ ☺ ☹	☺ ☺ ☹	☺ ☺ ☹
I understand the concepts of "hold the line" and "retreat the line" and evaluate the options	☺ ☺ ☹	☺ ☺ ☹	☺ ☺ ☹
I understand what SMPs (shaping shoreline management plans) are and how they work.	☺ ☺ ☹	☺ ☺ ☹	☺ ☺ ☹
I understand the government and LA roles in coastal SMP.	☺ ☺ ☹	☺ ☺ ☹	☺ ☺ ☹
I understand the different stakeholders' views and relate to a case study.	☺ ☺ ☹	☺ ☺ ☹	☺ ☺ ☹
I can explain how coastal flooding by sea levels and increased frequency of storms can be managed.	☺ ☺ ☹	☺ ☺ ☹	☺ ☺ ☹
I can describe and explain how the coastline in the UK and the Maldives (two different development coastline) is affected by climate change.	☺ ☺ ☹	☺ ☺ ☹	☺ ☺ ☹

Practice questions

1. Define the following terms:

   a) Geology

   ....
   ....

   b) Erosion

   ....
   ....

   c) Retreat

   ....
   ....

   (3 marks)

2. Explain how erosion breaks down material.

....
....
....
....

(2 marks)

3. Describe how resistant rock (hard) forms a headland.

....
....
....
....
....
....
....
....
....
....
....
....
....
....
....
....

(6 marks)

4. Draw and annotate a diagram of a spit.

(6 marks)

5. Name and describe the transportation methods.

....
....
....
....
....
....
....
....
....

(4 marks)

6. Name 3 methods of hard engineering and explain how each works.

....
....
....
....
....
....
....
....
....
....
....
....
....
....

(6 marks)

7. Explain 2 different methods of soft engineering and evaluate each one.

....
....
....
....
....
....
....
....
....
....
....
....
....
....
....

(6 marks)

8. Explain what a shoreline protection method is and their role.

....
....
....
....
....
....
....
....
....
....
....
....
....
....
....
....

(6 marks)

9. Explain how seasonal weather effects the coastline.

....
....
....
....
....
....
....
....
....
....
....

(4 marks)

10. Assess using an example how coastal landscapes and communities are affected by climate change.

....
....
....
....
....
....
....
....
....
....
....
....
....
....
....
....
....
....
....
....
....

(8 marks)

Key Idea 2.2: Shaping the landscape - rivers and river management

Knowledge Checklist

Specification statement These are the bits the exam board wants you to know, make sure you can do all of these…	Self-assessment		
	First review 4-7 months before exam	Second review 1-2 months before exam	Final review Week before exam
I can give the meaning of each of these terms: Interception, transpiration, infiltration, surface run-off and throughflow.	☺ ☺ ☹	☺ ☺ ☹	☺ ☺ ☹
I can give the meaning of each erosion term: hydraulic action, abrasion, attrition, and solution.	☺ ☺ ☹	☺ ☺ ☹	☺ ☺ ☹
I can give the meaning of each transport term: traction, saltation, suspension, and solution.	☺ ☺ ☹	☺ ☺ ☹	☺ ☺ ☹
I can describe the main features of each of the following river landforms: V–shaped valley, waterfall, gorge, meander, ox-bow lake, floodplain, estuary.	☺ ☺ ☹	☺ ☺ ☹	☺ ☺ ☹
I can describe the main processes that can change the shape of two river landforms.	☺ ☺ ☹	☺ ☺ ☹	☺ ☺ ☹
I can recall three facts about one flash flood that I studied.	☺ ☺ ☹	☺ ☺ ☹	☺ ☺ ☹
I can describe one type of hard engineering, and one type of soft engineering, used to manage rivers.	☺ ☺ ☹	☺ ☺ ☹	☺ ☺ ☹
I can explain why water moves through one drainage basin more quickly than another because of the geology	☺ ☺ ☹	☺ ☺ ☹	☺ ☺ ☹
I can explain why cutting down and planting trees can alter the stores/flows in a drainage basin.	☺ ☺ ☹	☺ ☺ ☹	☺ ☺ ☹
I can explain why building towns and roads can alter the stores/flows in a drainage basin.	☺ ☺ ☹	☺ ☺ ☹	☺ ☺ ☹

I can give two different reasons why people alter rivers.	☺ ☺ ☹	☺ ☺ ☹	☺ ☺ ☹
I can explain why flood risk can be reduced by: Building dams; changing river channels (e.g. dredging); and land-use zoning in towns.	☺ ☺ ☹	☺ ☺ ☹	☺ ☺ ☹
I can compare the shape of two contrasting hydrographs and use them to identify possible reasons for the differences in discharge that I have noted.	☺ ☺ ☹	☺ ☺ ☹	☺ ☺ ☹
I can identify a range of impacts of flooding and sort these into positive and negative; social and economic consequences.	☺ ☺ ☹	☺ ☺ ☹	☺ ☺ ☹
I can suggest why stakeholders (different groups of people) hold different views on river management and then explain why they have these views.	☺ ☺ ☹	☺ ☺ ☹	☺ ☺ ☹
I can evaluate social, economic and environmental costs and benefits of river management.	☺ ☺ ☹	☺ ☺ ☹	☺ ☺ ☹
I can make connections between the impact of river management in one place and the effects of the management further downstream.	☺ ☺ ☹	☺ ☺ ☹	☺ ☺ ☹
I can rank the effectiveness of different strategies that attempt to reduce the flood risk and evaluate them.	☺ ☺ ☹	☺ ☺ ☹	☺ ☺ ☹
I can use evidence to demonstrate why one river management strategy is more sustainable than another.	☺ ☺ ☹	☺ ☺ ☹	☺ ☺ ☹
I can make suggestions to reduce tension between different groups of people (stakeholders) when management decisions are controversial.	☺ ☺ ☹	☺ ☺ ☹	☺ ☺ ☹

Practice questions

1. Name two features in each section of a river course.

Upper	Middle	Lower

(6 marks)

2. Explain how a waterfall is formed with use of a series of diagrams.

(6 marks)

3. Draw and annotate a diagram of a river / drainage basin.

(6 marks)

4. Name and explain at least two human and two physical causes of flooding.

....
....
....
....
....
....
....
....
....
....
....
....

(4 marks)

5. Explain why people have altered a rivers course.

....
....
....
....

(2 marks)

6. Explain the causes and impacts of a flash flood that you have studied.

....
....
....
....
....
....
....
....
....
....
....
....
....
....
....
....
....
....
....
....
....

(8 marks)

7. Annotate the flood / storm hydrograph below and explain whether it is a flash flood or not and why.

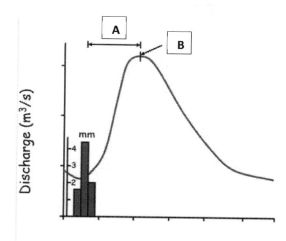

Hours from start of rain storm

....
....
....
....
....
....

(4 marks)

8. Name 3 impacts of flooding and sort these into positive and negative; social and economic consequences and explain each one.

....
....
....
....
....
....
....
....
....
....
....
....
....
....
....
....
....
....
....
....
....
....
....
....
....
....

(8 marks)

9. Explain the different methods of river management and how they reduce the risk of flooding.

....
....
....
....
....
....
....
....
....
....
....
....
....
....
....
....

(6 marks)

10. Evaluate the effectiveness of different strategies that attempt to reduce the flood risk and evaluate them.

....
....
....
....
....
....
....
....
....
....
....
....
....
....
....
....
....
....
....
....
....
....
....
....

(8 marks)

Key Idea 2.3: Weather and climate

Knowledge Checklist

Specification statement These are the bits the exam board wants you to know, make sure you can do all of these…	Self-assessment		
	First review 4-7 months before exam	Second review 1-2 months before exam	Final review Week before exam
I can give the meaning of each of these terms: Maritime climate, seasonality, precipitation, latitude, altitude, air pressure, weather, climate, continentality, isobar, drought.	☺ ☺ ☹	☺ ☺ ☹	☺ ☺ ☹
I can describe the distribution of world climates.	☺ ☺ ☹	☺ ☺ ☹	☺ ☺ ☹
I can describe the main features of the UK climate.	☺ ☺ ☹	☺ ☺ ☹	☺ ☺ ☹
I can locate and describe the key features of the hot semi-arid climate.	☺ ☺ ☹	☺ ☺ ☹	☺ ☺ ☹
I can locate and describe the key features of the equatorial climate.	☺ ☺ ☹	☺ ☺ ☹	☺ ☺ ☹
I can explain what the ITCZ is and remember three facts about the ITCZ.	☺ ☺ ☹	☺ ☺ ☹	☺ ☺ ☹
I can describe the weather associated with an anticyclone.	☺ ☺ ☹	☺ ☺ ☹	☺ ☺ ☹
I can describe the sequence of weather associated with the passing of a depression.	☺ ☺ ☹	☺ ☺ ☹	☺ ☺ ☹
I can explain the global atmospheric circulation model.	☺ ☺ ☹	☺ ☺ ☹	☺ ☺ ☹
I can explain why the UK has a mild, wet climate.	☺ ☺ ☹	☺ ☺ ☹	☺ ☺ ☹
I can explain how aspect, altitude, latitude, distance from the sea, prevailing wind, air masses and aspect affect temperature.	☺ ☺ ☹	☺ ☺ ☹	☺ ☺ ☹

I can explain how the ITCZ affects climate patterns.	☺ ☻ ☹	☺ ☻ ☹	☺ ☻ ☹
I can explain the formation of tropical storms.	☺ ☻ ☹	☺ ☻ ☹	☺ ☻ ☹
I can give two different reasons why high- and low-pressure systems bring different types of weather.	☺ ☻ ☹	☺ ☻ ☹	☺ ☻ ☹
I can explain how different groups of people were affected by the drought in California.	☺ ☻ ☹	☺ ☻ ☹	☺ ☻ ☹
I can explain how different groups of people were affected by a tropical storm studied (e.g. Hurricane Katerina)	☺ ☻ ☹	☺ ☻ ☹	☺ ☻ ☹
I can create links between the distribution of climates and the distribution of ecosystems.	☺ ☻ ☹	☺ ☻ ☹	☺ ☻ ☹
I can compare two contrasting climate graphs and use the evidence to identify possible reasons for the differences noted.	☺ ☻ ☹	☺ ☻ ☹	☺ ☻ ☹
Looking at an extreme weather events and I can sort the impacts into positive and negative; social, environmental and economic consequences.	☺ ☻ ☹	☺ ☻ ☹	☺ ☻ ☹
I can evaluate the relative short- and long-term consequences of extreme weather events.	☺ ☻ ☹	☺ ☻ ☹	☺ ☻ ☹
I can evaluate the strengths and weaknesses of strategies used to reduce the effects of extreme weather events.	☺ ☻ ☹	☺ ☻ ☹	☺ ☻ ☹
I can explain which effects from an extreme weather events, and rank the worst and explain why.	☺ ☻ ☹	☺ ☻ ☹	☺ ☻ ☹
I can predict the immediate and long-term needs of people suffering as a result of an extreme weather event.	☺ ☻ ☹	☺ ☻ ☹	☺ ☻ ☹
I can make suggestions to protect people from future devastation caused by an extreme weather event.	☺ ☻ ☹	☺ ☻ ☹	☺ ☻ ☹

Practice questions

1. Describe the distribution of the world climates and name examples.

....
....
....
....
....
....
....

(2 marks)

2. Describe the weather associated with an anticyclone and depression in both the summer and the winter.

....
....
....
....
....
....
....
....
....
....

(4 marks)

3. Explain the difference between the equatorial and semi-arid climates and explain why this happened.

....
....
....
....
....
....
....
....
....
....

(4 marks)

4. Explain the global atmospheric circulation model and how it impacts weather in different locations.

....
....
....
....
....
....
....
....
....
....
....
....
....
....
....
....
....

(6 marks)

5. Using an example, explain how different groups of people were affected by the drought.

....
....
....
....
....
....
....
....
....
....
....
....

(4 marks)

6. Explain why the UK has a mild, wet climate.

....
....
....
....
....
....
....

(2 marks)

7. Describe the links between the distribution of climates and the distribution of ecosystems.

....
....
....
....
....
....
....

(2 marks)

8. Explain the consequences of extreme weather events.

....
....
....
....
....
....
....
....
....
....
....
....

(4 marks)

9. Using the extreme weather event that you have studied, give 3 causes of the event and 3 impacts.

....
....
....
....
....
....
....
....
....
....
....
....
....
....
....
....
....
....

(6 marks)

10. Using the extreme weather event that you have studied, assess how the event impacted the people and environment.

....
....
....
....
....
....
....
....
....
....
....
....
....
....
....
....
....
....
....
....
....
....
....
....
....
....
....
....
....
....

(8 marks)

Key Idea 2.4: Climate change - cause and effect

Knowledge Checklist

Specification statement These are the bits the exam board wants you to know, make sure you can do all of these…	Self-assessment		
	First review 4-7 months before exam	Second review 1-2 months before exam	Final review Week before exam
I can describe how has climate changed during the Quaternary period.	☺ ☺ ☹	☺ ☺ ☹	☺ ☺ ☹
I can describe how climate has changed to include glacial and inter-glacial periods.	☺ ☺ ☹	☺ ☺ ☹	☺ ☺ ☹
I can name the processes that create the greenhouse effect.	☺ ☺ ☹	☺ ☺ ☹	☺ ☺ ☹
I can annotate a diagram of the greenhouse effect.	☺ ☺ ☹	☺ ☺ ☹	☺ ☺ ☹
I can explain the evidence for global warming.	☺ ☺ ☹	☺ ☺ ☹	☺ ☺ ☹
I can explain the role of human activity as one contributory factor in global warming	☺ ☺ ☹	☺ ☺ ☹	☺ ☺ ☹
I can explain the consequences of climate change for people and Environments.	☺ ☺ ☹	☺ ☺ ☹	☺ ☺ ☹
I can describe and explain the impact of climate change on coastal management strategies with the consequences on at least two: ○ Farming and food supply ○ Wildlife and habitats ○ Water and water supplies ○ Where people live and population movement ○ Tourism and tourist destinations.	☺ ☺ ☹	☺ ☺ ☹	☺ ☺ ☹
I can explain how and why do attitudes to climate change vary.	☺ ☺ ☹	☺ ☺ ☹	☺ ☺ ☹

I can use differing views, values and attitudes which are held on the issue of climate change and the ways in which its effects could be addressed.	☺ ☺ ☹	☺ ☺ ☹	☺ ☺ ☹
I can name and use global initiatives to reduce the impact of climate change.	☺ ☺ ☹	☺ ☺ ☹	☺ ☺ ☹
I can explain the role that individuals and government in the UK can play in reducing the risk of climate change?	☺ ☺ ☹	☺ ☺ ☹	☺ ☺ ☹
I can explain how individuals can play a part in reducing the risk of climate change.	☺ ☺ ☹	☺ ☺ ☹	☺ ☺ ☹
I can explain how and why local and national UK government may attempt to reduce the risk of climate change.	☺ ☺ ☹	☺ ☺ ☹	☺ ☺ ☹

Practice questions

1. Describe how climate has changed to include glacial and inter-glacial periods.

....
....
....
....
....

(2 marks)

2. Name one greenhouse gas.

....

(1 marks)

3. Describe the processes that create the greenhouse effect.

....
....
....
....
....
....
....
....
....
....
....
....

(4 marks)

4. Explain how increased meat consumption has impacted greenhouse gases.

....
....
....
....
....
....
....
....
....
....
....
....
....
....
....

(4 marks)

5. Explain one other human activity as **one** contributory factor in global warming.

....
....
....
....
....
....

(2 marks)

6. Describe how climate change affects tourism in one region you have studied.

....
....
....
....
....
....
....
....
....
....
....
....

(4 marks)

7. Describe the global initiatives to reduce the impact of climate change.

....
....
....
....
....
....
....
....
....
....
....
....

(4 marks)

8. Describe the initiatives that have already taken place in the UK.

....
....
....
....
....
....
....
....
....
....
....
....

(4 marks)

9. Explain the role that individuals and government in the UK can play in reducing the risk of climate change.

....
....
....
....
....
....
....
....
....
....
....
....

(4 marks)

10. Assess the way climate change affects water supply in one region.

....
....
....
....
....
....
....
....
....
....
....
....
....
....
....
....
....

(6 marks)

Theme 3: ENVIRONMENTAL CHALLENGES

Key Idea 3.1: How ecosystems function & Key Idea 3.2: Ecosystems under threat

Knowledge Checklist

Specification statement These are the bits the exam board wants you to know, make sure you can do all of these...	Self-assessment		
	First review 4-7 months before exam	Second review 1-2 months before exam	Final review Week before exam
I can give the meaning of each of the following: ecosystem, biodiversity, conservation.	☺ ☺ ☹	☺ ☺ ☹	☺ ☺ ☹
I can name and describe the location of two contrasting ecosystems.	☺ ☺ ☹	☺ ☺ ☹	☺ ☺ ☹
I can describe how farming methods can damage an ecosystem.	☺ ☺ ☹	☺ ☺ ☹	☺ ☺ ☹
I can describe and locate one ecosystem that is being managed.	☺ ☺ ☹	☺ ☺ ☹	☺ ☺ ☹
I can explain why food production methods change natural processes (like nutrient cycles) in an ecosystem.	☺ ☺ ☹	☺ ☺ ☹	☺ ☺ ☹
I can give reasons why energy or water resource production can have negative impacts on the environment.	☺ ☺ ☹	☺ ☺ ☹	☺ ☺ ☹
I can explain why sustainable management of food production is necessary in hot semi-arid grassland regions.	☺ ☺ ☹	☺ ☺ ☹	☺ ☺ ☹
I can explain links between local scale damage to ecosystems and wider regional consequences.	☺ ☺ ☹	☺ ☺ ☹	☺ ☺ ☹
Using the case study of one ecosystem you have studied, write a balanced summary of trends and changes shown in evidence and data.	☺ ☺ ☹	☺ ☺ ☹	☺ ☺ ☹

I can use sources such as table/graph/photograph/map to analysis the damage to ecosystem stability.	☺ ☺ ☹	☺ ☺ ☹	☺ ☺ ☹
I can select reliable data to highlight impact of food production on the environment.	☺ ☺ ☹	☺ ☺ ☹	☺ ☺ ☹
I can use evidence to demonstrate how poor land management has affected one region of hot semi-arid grassland.	☺ ☺ ☹	☺ ☺ ☹	☺ ☺ ☹
Looking at your case study, evaluate the outcomes of local scale conservation strategies.	☺ ☺ ☹	☺ ☺ ☹	☺ ☺ ☹
Explain why decisions to increase food production or energy production in vulnerable areas are difficult.	☺ ☺ ☹	☺ ☺ ☹	☺ ☺ ☹
I can use evidence to make recommendations on how a named ecosystem should be managed.	☺ ☺ ☹	☺ ☺ ☹	☺ ☺ ☹
I can use evidence to argue why sustainable management strategies are necessary in hot semi-arid grasslands.	☺ ☺ ☹	☺ ☺ ☹	☺ ☺ ☹
I can use evidence to shape an argument for sustainable conservation in a named ecosystem.	☺ ☺ ☹	☺ ☺ ☹	☺ ☺ ☹

Practice questions

1. Describe the location of two contrasting ecosystems.

....
....
....
....
....

(2 marks)

2. Explain why energy or water resource production can have negative impacts on the environment.

....
....
....
....
....
....
....
....
....
....
....
....

(4 marks)

3. Demonstrate how poor land management has affected one region of hot semi-arid grassland.

....
....
....
....
....
....
....
....
....
....

(4 marks)

4. What are 'buttress roots' and why are they necessary?

....
....
....
....

(2 marks)

5. Define the following terms:

   a) Consumer

   ....
   ....

   b) Tertiary

   ....
   ....

   c) Biotic

   ....
   ....

                                                                              (3 marks)

6. Trees in tropical rainforests have adapted to their biome. What does adaptation mean?

   ....
   ....
   ....
   ....

                                                                              (2 marks)

7. What are the impacts of human exploitation of your chosen ecosystem? Consider environmental, social and economic.

....
....
....
....
....
....
....
....
....
....
....
....
....

(6 marks)

8. Looking at your case study, evaluate the outcomes of local scale conservation strategies.

....
....
....
....
....
....
....
....
....
....
....
....
....
....
....
....
....
....
....
....

(8 marks)

9. Describe and explain the main threats to the hot semi-arid grassland.

....
....
....
....
....
....
....
....
....
....
....
....
....
....
....
....
....
....
....
....
....
....

(8 marks)

10. Assess the sustainable management strategies necessary in hot semi-arid grasslands.

....
....
....
....
....
....
....
....
....
....
....
....
....
....
....
....
....
....
....
....
....
....
....
....
....

(8 marks)

Key Idea 3.3: Water resources and management

Knowledge Checklist

Specification statement These are the bits the exam board wants you to know, make sure you can do all of these...	Self-assessment		
	First review 4-7 months before exam	Second review 1-2 months before exam	Final review Week before exam
I can define the following terms: water surplus, water deficit, water footprint, water transfer, water storage.	☺ ☺ ☹	☺ ☺ ☹	☺ ☺ ☹
I can describe the past and present global trends in water supply, the concept of water footprints and security.	☺ ☺ ☹	☺ ☺ ☹	☺ ☺ ☹
I can evaluate the social, economic and environmental reasons why demand and supply changes over time and place.	☺ ☺ ☹	☺ ☺ ☹	☺ ☺ ☹
I can explain the links between population change, economic growth, consumerism and demand for water.	☺ ☺ ☹	☺ ☺ ☹	☺ ☺ ☹
I can explain the concept of over-abstraction and the reasons for water transfer scheme.	☺ ☺ ☹	☺ ☺ ☹	☺ ☺ ☹
I can explain the impact of over-abstraction on people, the economy and the environment	☺ ☺ ☹	☺ ☺ ☹	☺ ☺ ☹
Case study: The Colorado River (USA& Mexico) The ways in which an imbalance of water supply can be met within one country (USA)	☺ ☺ ☹	☺ ☺ ☹	☺ ☺ ☹
The international issues facing water management across international boundaries (USA and Mexico)	☺ ☺ ☹	☺ ☺ ☹	☺ ☺ ☹

Practice questions

1. Define the following terms:

    Water footprint

    ....
    ....

    Water storage.

    ....
    ....

    (2 marks)

2. Explain the changing demands for water in the last 100 years.

    ....
    ....
    ....
    ....
    ....
    ....
    ....
    ....
    ....
    ....
    ....
    ....
    ....
    ....
    ....
    ....

    (4 marks)

3. Explain the link between population change and economic growth.

....
....
....
....
....
....
....
....
....
....
....
....
....

(4 marks)

4. Describe the concept of over-abstraction and the impact this has on areas.

....
....
....
....
....
....
....
....
....
....
....
....

(4 marks)

5. Explain the need for a water transfer scheme.

....
....
....
....
....
....
....
....
....
....
....
....

(4 marks)

6. Studying your case study, explain the needs for the water transfer scheme and the impact on the environment and the people.

....
....
....
....
....
....
....
....
....
....
....
....
....
....
....
....
....
....
....
....
....
....

(8 marks)

Key Idea 3.4: Desertification

Knowledge Checklist

Specification statement These are the bits the exam board wants you to know, make sure you can do all of these...	Self-assessment		
	First review 4-7 months before exam	Second review 1-2 months before exam	Final review Week before exam
I can describe the location and distribution of environments vulnerable to desertification	☺ ☺ ☹	☺ ☺ ☹	☺ ☺ ☹
I can describe how this pattern is changing over time	☺ ☺ ☹	☺ ☺ ☹	☺ ☺ ☹
I can explain how desertification is related to the global circulation of the atmosphere and the dominance of high-pressure systems.	☺ ☺ ☹	☺ ☺ ☹	☺ ☺ ☹
I can explain how changing climatic patterns over a long time has led to unreliable rainfall patterns and higher rates of evapotranspiration in hot semi-arid regions.	☺ ☺ ☹	☺ ☺ ☹	☺ ☺ ☹
I can explain how changing patterns of vegetation can lead to desertification	☺ ☺ ☹	☺ ☺ ☹	☺ ☺ ☹
I can explain how evapotranspiration can lead to desertification	☺ ☺ ☹	☺ ☺ ☹	☺ ☺ ☹
I can explain how micro-climates can lead to desertification	☺ ☺ ☹	☺ ☺ ☹	☺ ☺ ☹
I can explain how human activity can lead to drought including: Unsustainable use of water resources Over-grazing Poor land management Use of firewood	☺ ☺ ☹	☺ ☺ ☹	☺ ☺ ☹

I can give the different viewpoints values and attitudes of stakeholders in regions which are vulnerable to desertification	☺ ☺ ☹	☺ ☺ ☹	☺ ☺ ☹
I can give examples of a range of strategies used by NGOs (Non-governmental organizations) working at a local level with communities including: Drip irrigation Magic stones Use of drought tolerant crops	☺ ☺ ☹	☺ ☺ ☹	☺ ☺ ☹
I can give examples of international strategies aimed at reducing the spread of areas experiencing desertification	☺ ☺ ☹	☺ ☺ ☹	☺ ☺ ☹

Practice questions

1. Define the following terms:

Hot desert

....
....
....
....

Over-grazing

....
....
....
....

(2 marks)

2. Explain how desertification is related to the global circulation of the atmosphere and the dominance of high-pressure systems.

....
....
....
....
....
....
....
....
....
....
....
....

(4 marks)

3. Explain how changing patterns of vegetation can lead to desertification.

....
....
....
....
....
....
....
....
....
....
....
....

(4 marks)

4. Explain how economic development has increased desertification.

....
....
....
....
....
....
....
....
....
....
....
....
....
....
....

(6 marks)

5. Explain at least two strategies used with local communities to manage the problems of desertification.

....
....
....
....
....
....
....
....
....
....
....
....

(4 marks)

6. Explain two international strategies and the impact on desertification.

....
....
....
....
....
....
....
....
....
....
....
....

(4 marks)

Case Study Booklet

Case studies – An Introduction

Within your lessons you will have seen many examples that your teachers have used to strengthen your understanding of issues - it is much easier to understand an issue if you can visualise it.

You do not have to revise all of these examples in a huge amount of detail. However, you do need to know a few case studies in detail. This workbook contains examples of case studies that you can learn in depth and use. This is important to help you achieve the top marks in the extended questions, which are level marked.

What is the difference between a case study and example?

If a question asks for an example, that is all that is required; it can be as simple as just providing a named place.

By contrast for a case study, you need to know and demonstrate a depth of knowledge (including key facts and figures) and apply this when answering the question.

Depending on your specification, you will need to know at least one from each topic. There are multiple examples in each category – depending on your case study requirement – **YOU DO NOT NEED TO KNOW EACH ONE!**

Ideally case studies should be recent, however some older examples are so unique that they are still applicable. You are unlikely to be penalised for using an older case study. Basically – if the case study answers the question – its fine.

This booklet does not contain all possible case studies, some specific examples will be local based on work that you have done in lessons connected to fieldwork.

Each exam board has produced generic level marks scheme which then have specific points to each question within for teachers / examiners. See section below on Exam board specifications for more information.

Case Study Questions

They are likely to be a mixture of "using an example" and "with reference to a case study". There is a difference:

Example = illustrates the point e.g. how coastal landforms are created.

Case study = wants a discussion / depth of point to show your understanding of multiple issues.

Examples of Case Study Questions

1. Assess how people have impacted the environment within one biome you have studied.

2. Discuss the impacts of a tropical storm that you have studied.

3. Evaluate the success of sustainable methods used within one ecosystem you have studied.

4. Explain the social and environmental impacts that the overseas investment has had on the country or region.

5. Analysis the impact TNC / MNC have had on both the host and country of origin.

6. Asses the influence of global cites on the region surrounding.

How to answer a case study

Look at the example below of a question:

"Discuss the impact a TNC has on your LIC / NEE."

Firstly:

You need to decode / break the question down. One technique that is often used by successful candidates is to work backwards within your plan:

> **NEE / LIC** - *India*
> **TNC** – *TATA steel* (also called MNC – Multi National Cooperation)
> **IMPACT** – *effects positive / negatives* **DISCUSS** – you need to look at both sides and debate it.
> There is enough room at the side of the page (or even those pages with "this page is deliberately left blank" to create a plan.

Secondly:

Only include the information that answers this question. Do not drift and give lots of facts. You will need to be concise as you only have 10 min at most to answer this question.

Command words:

Make sure you know what the question wants and don't get into the trap of "case study dump" whereby candidates put down everything they've learnt about a case study.

Look at the following key information and consider

- Which would you include?
- Why?
- Make sure it is relevant to the question – don't include just for the sake of it!

> **Information**
> - India largest population
> - Airport – hub so makes it more well known
> - 60th largest company in the world
> - Recycling in Dharavi – 85% of Mumbai waste – well known around the world for this.
> - TATA accounts for over 3% of India's GDP
> - Headquarters are in Mumbai – unusual for a MNC
> - Large working population – youthful population – 10% of all factory employed, 40% of income tax is generated in Mumbai
> - Rapid growth of Bollywood – more worldwide, films including Slumdog Millionaire increases its influence
> - Stock exchange located
> - TATA steel headquarters and other shipping
> - TATA operates in over 100 countries.
> - National park within the city – this promotes wellbeing, but also shows how planning can work.
> - New industries within the city including medical research

What you need to know for the exam?

You do not need to know every detail – far from it. However, do not make facts up! Examiners are teachers too and they will know most case studies!

If you do struggle to remember facts in the exam – **DO NOT PANIC!**

Sentences such as:

- The death toll in Hurricane Katrina was only 3.   NO

- The death toll from Hurricane Katrina was over 1800.   WILL BE ACCEPTED

- The death toll from Hurricane Katrina was exactly 1836   WILL BE ACCEPTED

- The death toll was 3000 from Hurricane Katrina.   NO

It is important that you use a few facts but structure the answer effectively to achieve as higher marks as possible.

Structuring your answer

Structure Strips

This is a technique that looks at breaking down the question and trying to ensure you have covered it all. There are typically 5 parts for any question that requires the use of a case study. Here is an example:

"Discuss the impact a TNC has on your LIC / NEE."

Introduction
This is where you need to name your TNC and your LIC / NEE. Give a brief outline over the TNC and country (e.g. LIC is in North Africa and has seen a shift towards secondary industry which is where TNC (named) has established there.)

Impact 1
- Use sentence starts such as "One impact is" and use one fact / evidence.
- Make sure you use connectors such as
       "this affects the environment / people / businesses"
       "this is a challenge because it means"
       "this results in... "
       "this leads to..."

However
Lead to the second impact – possibly switch positive / negative.

Impact 2
- Look at a second impact, switch from people to environment or people to businesses.
- Use sentence starts such as "A further impact is" and use one fact / evidence.
- Make sure you use connectors such as
       "this affects the environment / people / businesses"
       "this is a challenge because it means"
       "this results in... "

Conclusion
Summaries the points you have discussed – remember this is the command word!
Give a reason e.g. "I believe this" "in summary"

P.E.E.L

This focuses on ensure you use the right connectives in your answer to structure the answer. Here are some examples of the connectives:

Point
- On the one hand...
- In addition...
- It is clear...
- Furthermore...

Evidence
- This is supported by...
- It can be seen in...
- For example...
- This is demonstrated...
- Using the source A it shows...

Explain
- As a result...
- This shows that...
- This suggests that...
- This leads me to believe...
- This means...
- Therefore it can be argued

Link
- It is clear that ...
- The most important factor ...
- Significantly, the factor that ...
- In conclusion...
- In summary...

Examples

Short level questions

Example 1

Explain, using an example why people in High Income Countries (HIC) continue to live in areas affected by tectonic hazards.

(4 marks)

A

One of the main reasons, as seen in Italy, is farmland. For example, the fields around Mt Etna are very fertile and farming is very successful. Another reason why people still live near volcanoes in HIC is tourism. People like to visit the volcano and tour guides have a good business, like in Iceland.

B

People live in HIC like New Zealand because there isn't much of a risk and there are engineering jobs in trying to protect buildings from tectonic activity.

C

Tectonic hazards occur in HIC. However, as the technology and access resources are easier, it is easier to live in these areas. Technology such as the warning systems used in Japan, which gave 90 seconds warning of the 2011 Tsunami, and with schools having regular earthquake drills, many people feel safe in this knowledge. Tectonic areas also bring positive economic opportunities such as geothermal energy as seen in New Zealand, which provide not only employment but also income for the government. As a result, the threats of tectonic events are not seen as big compared to LIC.

Comments on Example 1:

This question is more about the reasons rather than the example, however without an example you cannot achieve the highest level.

A:

Uses clearly reasons about why people live in tectonic hazards and it also two appropriate examples of countries (Mt Etna (Italy), and Iceland), this would score the higher marks.

B:

On the other hand, B is brief and a little basic but at most would achieve half marks as it does use appropriate examples.

C:

This is a stronger answer with examples linked to HIC. This would achieve full marks due to the linking to the examples to the question.

Example 2

Explain the impact of a tectonic event with use of an example.

(4 marks)

> **A**
>
> Volcanoes are rare but dangerous events, like Montserrat in 1995-1997. It really affected people in many ways including death (19 in Montserrat's case), people forced to live in evacuation camps and loss of farmland and jobs, which is really bad in LIC as they often have no benefits to help them out.

> **B**
>
> Volcanoes are hazards that can really have an impact on people. They can affect people in many different ways including roads being destroyed making it difficult for help to arrive. Also people can die like they did in Montserrat.

> **C**
>
> Volcanoes are really bad to a local area. People can die and can end up evacuated. It is really bad for them.

Comments on Example 2:

A:

Very clear answer with key information with link to impacts. This would score ¾ - to improve it further would need another evidence / fact to support the impacts.

B:

Far too vague, not really specific. At most would score 1 /4.

C:

This is not specific to an example and would not unlikely be credited.

Example 3:

Using an area of coastline that you have studied, explain how the landforms have been created.

(6 marks)

A

The coastline I have studied is the Dorset Coastline – Jurassic coastline. There it has a number of features including:

Swanage - headland and bay

Durdle Door – sea arch

Chesil Beach – bar.

The Old Harry rocks (stack stump) formed because the headland is the rocky coastline that sticks into the sea. It is a combination of resistant and less resistant rocks. The areas where there are fewer resistant rocks see erosion happening, which creates bays.

B

There are a number of features on the coastline which form because of a number of reasons, the biggest being the geology of the area. As the coastline is hit by the prevailing winds, they weaken the rocks. In areas with softer rock such as boulder clay, the cliffs collapse into the shoreline by slumping and bays are created in areas where there are fewer resistant rocks. In areas where the coastline has resistant rocks such as limestone, there are a number of features formed. One example is a cave. The waves erode small cracks and breaks into a small cave. Once this happens the rocks become vulnerable and it gets broken the whole way through to form an arch. As the rocks become unstable above, it collapses leaving behind a column. As this is on its own, it is very vulnerable and is eroded further into stump and eventually is completing washed away.

C

The Holderness coastline is a very famous coastline for having distinctive landforms. At Flamborough head there is a clear wave notch which as the waves continue to erode, the cliffs above become very fragile and eventually collapse as the cliffs are unstable. There is evidence of the following features: stacks, stumps and wave cut platforms.

Comments on Example 3:

This question is more about the landforms have been created. There are a number of things to considered, especially as it's a 6 mark question.

Examples need to be appropriate, using a minimum of 2 examples with explanation. Step by step isn't needed, but an overview of the formation is needed.

A:

Good overview but not enough detail = unlikely to achieve more than 2 marks.

B:

Clear answer with some detail, no more than 4 marks as it doesn't use a named example! Don't make this mistake!!!!

C:

Appropriate example but basic (level 1 only), achieves only 1, maybe 2 marks.

Extended question

Example 4:

Assess how a weather event caused by low pressure affected people.

(8 marks)

(9 marks – AQA only)

A

Weather events that are caused by low pressure differ around the world. In the UK this is caused by a depression and gives wet, windy and unsettled weather. Occasionally this causes flash flooding, especially around high tides as seen during Storm Desmond.

However in countries around the equator, tropical storms form from the high sea temperatures. This creates large storms with very high winds and rainfall. In the USA, the tropical storm called Hurricane Katrina hit in 2005. It caused over 1800 deaths, mainly among the poor black community and ageing sections of the population. The levees failed, despite the fact that the authorities knew they were old and poor. Many people moved out of city and as a result the city became even more run down.

B

Hurricane Katrina hit the USA city of New Orleans in 2005. It caused the following:

- 200 mph winds hit the coast – bringing down power lines and leaving 100,000 without electricity.

- A Storm Surge of 9m flooded in towards the low-lying city, swamping the coastal areas and submerging houses. People escaped into upper floors of houses, into roof spaces or onto roofs.

- The death toll was over 1,800.

- Hurricane Katrina caused $100 billion in property damages.

C

Hurricane Katrina – New Orleans, USA 2005

The hurricane was a very powerful with winds over 175mph. It lashed the city and the tidal surge broke the levees and flooded the poorest part of the city. As a result of the storm and the slow response by the government over 1400 people died, most from the poorest areas. The hurricane also showed the world the USA's ethnicity issues as the majority were of the black community. Most people lost their homes and jobs and many permanently relocated to other areas.

Hurricanes are examples of powerful depressions formed as a result of warm sea temperatures (over 27), the closeness to the equator and the summer months. They develop as the warm air rises and draws up water vapour. As it condenses it release huge amounts of heat energy which powers the storm. Hurricanes loos their power as it travels over land. Hurricane Katrina was an example of a category 5 hurricane – the most powerful.

D

Weather events have a varied level of intensity and as a result the impact affects people in different ways. Tropical storms are one low pressure event that can have significant impact on people.

Hurricane Katrina was a category 5 storm that hit New Orleans and surrounding areas in 2005. Despite the USA being one of the wealthiest and powerful countries in the world, the tropical storm had a devastating impact on people. Firstly, over 1800 people died. This is significant as the storm was well known due to the forecasting technology used. One of the biggest reasons for the high death toll was that the poorest communities were unable to evacuate. Over 80% of people were evacuated but of those who stayed, 93% were black, who were the poorest. This suggests that social economic grouping had a part to play. Secondly the levees failed which caused extensive flooding (over 80% of the city) despite the fact the Government had known that the levees were unlikely to withstand a powerful hurricane. It is clear that the death toll could have been reduced had more people been evacuated.

Further affects included the economic cost of over $81billion in property damage and the loss of thousands of jobs as companies relocated away from New Orleans.

In conclusion, tropical storms which are an example of a low-pressure system can have widespread and significant impact on people.

Comments on Example 4:

This is the extended answer which would have SPAG added on (different exam boards have slightly different mark schemes).

Both clearly identify the case study with key accurate data. However neither fully answer the question on **assessing**.

A:

Doesn't really focus on the question until towards half way in the second paragraph. This would be just into Level 1 – despite it sounding fairly well.

B:

This is more a case study drop – just using lots of facts which would get top of Level 1. Not ideal but if you struggle in the exam, it's better to write something (even bullet points) than to leave it empty!

C:

This would hit over half marks despite having a few facts (one that is not accurate – death toll). It doesn't fully answer the question but has valid attempts at assessing.

D:

This is well structured, uses a few key parts of the case study but doesn't focus on the actual storm rather than the affects. This answer would achieve Level 4 marks.

You must on an **Assess** question (same on **evaluate** and **discuss**) add a summary / conclusion!!!

Exam board specifications

Eduqas B
Knowledge checklist

Case Study Requirement	Self-assessment		
	First review 4-7 months before exam	**Second review** 1-2 months before exam	**Final review** Week before exam
Global cities ○ one HIC inc sustainable strategies, transport, MNC role, Leisure use is managed	☺ ☺ ☹	☺ ☺ ☹	☺ ☺ ☹
Global cities ○ LIC / NIC inc slum clearance, MNC	☺ ☺ ☹	☺ ☺ ☹	☺ ☺ ☹
Aid: ○ **one** long-term development, ○ **one** short-term emergency, ○ both donor and LIC	☺ ☺ ☹	☺ ☺ ☹	☺ ☺ ☹
Climate change ○ one HIC	☺ ☺ ☹	☺ ☺ ☹	☺ ☺ ☹
Climate change ○ one LIC	☺ ☺ ☹	☺ ☺ ☹	☺ ☺ ☹
Weather – outside the UK ○ High pressure system.	☺ ☺ ☹	☺ ☺ ☹	☺ ☺ ☹
Weather – outside the UK ○ Low intense low pressure system.	☺ ☺ ☹	☺ ☺ ☹	☺ ☺ ☹
River – look at the landforms and rates of change are significantly different	☺ ☺ ☹	☺ ☺ ☹	☺ ☺ ☹
Coastal - look at the landforms and rates of change are significantly different	☺ ☺ ☹	☺ ☺ ☹	☺ ☺ ☹
Flooding: UK	☺ ☺ ☹	☺ ☺ ☹	☺ ☺ ☹
Ecosystem ○ Semi Arid grassland (core)	☺ ☺ ☹	☺ ☺ ☹	☺ ☺ ☹
Ecosystem ○ One other biome – Rainforest	☺ ☺ ☹	☺ ☺ ☹	☺ ☺ ☹
Ecosystem ○ One small scale ecosystem in the UK	☺ ☺ ☹	☺ ☺ ☹	☺ ☺ ☹

Mark scheme

Mark	Link https://www.eduqas.co.uk/qualifications/geography/gcse-b/GCSE-Geog-B-SAMs.pdf
4	Page 33
6	Page 32
8	Page 34

1. Case Studies - Weather

1.1 - Hurricane Katrina, August 2005

Location:

- USA
- Its main effects were in the southern states of Louisiana, Mississippi and Alabama.
- One particular hit city was New Orleans.

Storm:

- The hurricane was predicted and known to be a category 5 storm.
- Hurricane Katrina was the largest and 3rd strongest hurricane ever recorded to make landfall in the US.
- Katrina peaked at a Category 5 hurricane, with winds up to 175 mph.
- The storm surge from Katrina was 20-ft (six meters) high.

Effects:

- The final death toll was at 1,836, primarily from Louisiana (1,577) and Mississippi (238).
- Hurricane Katrina affected over 15 million people in different ways
- An estimated 80% of New Orleans was under water, up to 20 ft deep in places.
- Hurricane Katrina caused $81 billion in property damages
- Hurricane Katrina impacted about 90,000 square miles.
- More than 70 countries pledged monetary donations or other assistance after the hurricane.

Causes of the high death toll and cost:

- Over 80% of people were evacuated but of those who stayed, 93% were black.
- More than half of these victims were senior citizens.
- The government knew the levees were old and inadequate. They knew if they flooded it would cause 80% of the city to flood.
- The government knew that the black poor community of downtown and the elderly could not afford to leave the city.

1.2 - Typhoon Haiyan, November 2013.

Location:

- Philippines, South East Asia

Storm:

- Rainfall recorded up to 281.9 mm in 12 hours.
- Winds sustained winds of 195 mph and gusts up to 235 mph
- Storm surges of up tp 7m high.

Effects:

- Over 7000 people died with more than 27000 people injured.
- Almost 2 million people made homeless.
- Diseases spread quickly due to the lack of sanitation and contaminated water.
- Land damaged by landslides, contamination (oil in particular) and trees uprooted.

Long term:

- Almost £4 billion damage
- The areas most affected were farmland – over 71000 hectors damaged. This was where rice, corn and sugar-producing occurred, which was damaged.
- Warning systems had reduced the potential death toll due to the waning.
- Relief aid worth over £480 million was raised.

1.3 - Storm Desmond, December 2015

Location:

- UK

Causes:

- Rainfall in this storm broke all previous UK records including Honister in Cumbria received 341.4mm (13.4in) of rain
- Increased building on floodplain including around Cockermouth
- Heavy rain fell on land that had already been saturated in Cumbria.

Impact on people:

- Homeless: temporary accommodation costs - the government helped by providing local authorities with over £500 for each household affected.
- Over 60,000 homes without power. this means families forced to evacuate, unable to live in their homes, unsafe to cook etc.
- One person died in Cumbria and about 40 schools closed in Cumbria.
- Rail services disrupted which means people experienced delays or cancellations which impacts on being able to get to work etc.
- Cost over £760 million in insurance claims. Some homes at risk of not being able to get insurance or certainly not affordable insurance.

Some of the impacts on the environment:

- Rivers were significantly altered with increased rates of erosion.
- Landslides and mudslides were reported e.g. on the A83 at Rest and Be Thankful
- Soil contamination

1.4 - Attica Wildfires, July 2018

Location:

- Greek Mainland around the port town of Rafina, in particular Kokkino Limanaki and Mati. (North of Athens – 15km

Cause of the wildfire:

- Drought: began July 2018
- Dry winter and a hot summer where temperatures have risen above 40^C.
- High winds of up to 60mph spread the fire

Responses:

- Greece deployed its entire fleet of fire-fighting aircraft
- Over 250 fire engines and 600 firefighters
- EU Civil Protection Mechanism – organised assistance from other countries including water-tanker planes from Italy, Cyprus and Spain.

Impact on people:

- 100 people were confirmed dead and over 164 adults and 23 children injured.
- 700 residents evacuated and over 650 children from a summer camp
- Bodies lay just 15m (50ft) from the sea
- 1,500 homes had been damaged and many had been destroyed.
- No electricity days later due to the damage.
- Tourism dropped following

1.5 - Great Australia Drought, 2002-2009

Location:

- The south-east of Australia

Causes:

- El Niño – this is where the reversal of the moist trade winds mean rainfall is significantly reduced.
- Demand for water increased dramatically in the last 30 years together with population increase in the region.

Responses:

- Government restriction on use of water – enforced strongly in some areas.
- Desalination plants established
- Introduction of drought-tolerant plant species – despite the Australian Government tough rules on ecological issues - induction of new species.

Impact on people:

- Farmers struggle to make an income as livestock died and crop yields decreased.
- Wine industry affected – reduced income and tax generated for the government

Impact on the environment:

- Frequency of bushfires / wildfires increased
- Dams build in order to ensure water needs meet.

2. Case Studies – Ecosystems

2.1 - Amazon Rainforest, multiple examples

If you have not watched them – highly recommend Bruce Parry 2007 Amazon series.

Issues:

- Problems started with the building of the Trans Amazonia highway – was built to open up the rainforest for investment and access. Around 80% of all destruction of the Amazon comes 30km of an official road.

Cattle ranching:

- Clearance of the forest to graze the cattle/cows, most of which are then exported to USA (280m in 2009)
- A lot of the land has been illegally "purchased", new roads built to move the cattle and ports created along the rivers to move the cattle.
- Growth in the industry due to the fact Brazil is a NEE / NIC and the population is eating more red meat (link to climate change) and the meat is exported to generate income.

Gold mining:

- Clear the forest then use water to loosen the soil to find the gold, which means it spoils the rivers.
- This is almost always illegal, putting ingenious communities at risk with the pollution in the rivers as well as the impact of the noise from the mining.

Drugs:

- Manufacture of the drug cocaine involves cutting down forest to grow the coca plants.
- Rivers are polluted with the chemicals they use to make cocaine, like bleach and chlorine.
- Again this is illegal and puts pressure on indigenous communities from pollution.

Logging – selective:

- Cutting down specific types of tree, but normally involves losing 5 additional trees for every desired tree that is felled.
- Can mean a tree type becomes extinct.

Logging – commercial:

- Cutting down whole patches, can be as much as 60 football pitches a minute.

Indigenous communities:

- Vulnerable to outside disease (hepatitis, chickenpox and flu)
- Have historically been exploited in terms of land rights, pollution and some extent slavery.
- Now have protection, however this is not always enforceable.

Enforcing the law:

- High levels of corruption, difficult in the remoteness to enforce the law and only 12 police officers for an area the size of France.

2.2 – Greenland

If you have not watched them – highly recommend Bruce Parry Arctic series – Greenland episode.

- Over 80% of the Greenland is ice capped, meaning that it is covered with ice all year round.

- Greenland has a population of roughly 57,000, about 15,000 of whom live in the capital Nuuk.

- Scientists have estimated that the Greenland ice sheet is between 400,000 and 800,000 years old.

- The country is geographically part of North America, but politically is part of Europe.

- Growing evidence that climate change is impacting the traditional way of life – e.g. restrictions on hunting due to the declining numbers e.g. narwhal fin, polar bears.

- New resources such as Zinc have been discovered and are now being mined for commercial purposes.

3. Case Studies - Tectonics

3.1 - La-Aquila Earthquake, April 2009

Location:

- L'Aquila is a town region of Abruzzo, in central Italy.
- It is located on the major fault line that runs across the Apennine mountain range.

Details:

- 6.3 on the Richter scale occurred 3.32am.
- Rock fall and landslides.
- San Salvatore Hospital west wing collapse despite being built in 2000, under new building regulations.
- Several aftershocks measured around 5 on the Richter scale.

Impacts:

- Just over 300 people died (mainly from collapsed buildings) and around 1500 people were injured.
- Around 70,000 were made homeless and camps were set up with water, food and medical care.
- Estimated that the earthquake cost Italy $15 billion.

Responses:

- Seismologist were monitoring the area prior to the event.
- Many including the government and local residents felt that the scientist failed to predict the earthquake.
- 7 of these scientists were convicted of manslaughter but the convictions were later quashed in 2014.

3.2 - Bam Earthquake, December 2003

Location:

- Bam is a city and capital of Bam County, Kerman Province, in Iran.
- It is located near the major fault line that runs across Iran where the Arabian tectonic plate contacts the Eurasian plate.

Details:

- 6.5 on the Richter Scale with the depth of focus 10 km
- Occurred at 5.26am

Immediate Impacts:

- More than 26,000 people were killed, 50,000 were injured and 100,000 were made homeless.
- Roads, telephone lines and electricity cables were damaged. This slowed down the rescue attempts.
- Fissures (cracks) formed in the ground.
- Landslides and rock falls
- Lack of irrigation led to the death of many date and palm trees.
- The ground collapsed above underground irrigation channels.

Responses:

- 400,000 read-to-eat meals were provided, along with bread, rice, sugar and other food items to the homeless.
- Iranian Red Crescent arranged more than 8,500 relief workers, but many thought this wasn't enough.
- Fresh drinking water was not available until a month after the earthquake.

3.3 – Eyjafjallajökull volcano, March 2010

Location:

- Iceland
- The volcano has an ice cap cover the caldera of a volcano 1666m in height.

Impact on local people:

- Remote area, but over 800 people, mostly farmers evacuated overnight
- Some roads were closed because of a fear of flash floods due to the melting of the glaciers.
- These ash falls, which coated agricultural land with a thick layer of ash.

Impacts worldwide:

- Ash cloud had a massive impact due to the polar jet stream.
- For 8 day, over 100,000 flights were cancelled.
- Shut down of the airspace cost airlines an estimated £1.2bn and the cost to the economy was over £80 million.
- Many people discovered that their travel insurance did not cover natural hazards.
- Perishable foods and products were wasted as they could not be transported – Kenya farmers were affected by flowers dying as they were unable to reach the UK – over 3000 tonnes a day.

3.4 - Soufriere Hills volcano, 1995-1997

Location:

- Caribbean island of Montserrat
- The island lies on a destructive plate boundary where the North and South American plates are subduction beneath the Caribbean Plate.

Details:

- Eruption started on 18th of July 1995 and peaked in 1997.

Additional information:

- Ruled by the UK government as an overseas territory. This gives the people of Monserrate the right to live in the UK.
- Although it is classed as a LIC it does have some financial support from the UK which was vital in this case.
- The UK was the biggest receiver of those who left the islands.
- The eruptions were frequency for 2 years.
- Volcano erupted pyroclastic flow – the deadliest eruption.

Impact:

- Population fell from 12,000 in 1995 to 1,500 by 2001 (now slowly starting to rise again).
- Housing shortages leading to a 70% increase in rents – further hardship for islanders.
- 19 deaths and over 100 injured and 7 villages destroyed.
- 5,000 people evacuated to the safe zone to the north of the island.
- Evacuees living for a long time in cramped, unhygienic conditions in 'temporary' camps.
- Local people grew frustrated by the length of time evacuated and it had a large impact on the economy due to productivity falling from agriculture being restricted (due to access to the land).
- Damage to infrastructure made relief effort difficult – airport and main ports shut. The capital city Plymouth was evacuated permanently.
- Seen as overall success in terms of management due to the low death toll. Monitoring was seen as the key reason for this - it was established following the Nevado del Ruiz eruption (1985).

4. Case Studies - Rivers

4.1 - Boscastle flood, August 2004

Location:

- Villages of Cornwall and Crackington Haven in Cornwall, UK
- River Valency in the Valency valley, enters the sea at the harbour village of Boscastle.

Causes:

- Over 60 mm of rainfall (typically a month's rainfall) fell in two hours.
- The ground was already saturated due to the previous two weeks of above average rainfall.
- The drainage basin has many steep slopes, and has areas of impermeable slate causing rapid surface runoff.
- Boscastle is at the confluence (where tributaries meet) of three rivers - Valency, Jordan, and Paradise. A large quantity of water all arrived within a short space of time causing the rivers to overflow (falling trees also blocked the narrow bridges – human cause).
- The flooding coincided with a high tide, making the impact worse.

Effects:

- Homes, businesses and cars belonging to more than 1,000 people were swept away.
- Income from tourism was lost. This had an impact on livelihoods and the local economy.
- There were vast numbers of subsequent insurance claims. (estimated total cost of £500 Million).
- No lives were lost, partly due to the rapid response of the emergency services.

Subsequent management:

- New flood defence scheme cost £10 million and was finished in 2008.
- New wider bridge built and river made wider and deeper to accommodate rising levels after storm events (hard engineering).
- The National Trust and Environment Agency are restoring previously straightened sections to a more natural path that will allow deposition and slow the flow of the river (soft engineering).

4.2 - Somerset Levels floods, winter 2013-2014

Location:

- Somerset Levels, a coastal plain area in central Somerset, UK.

Background:

- Are only about 8m above sea level.
- Historically flooded twice a month from high tides until Romans built sea defences and also dredged the channels to improve drainage (turned into productive farmland).
- Coastal flooding affected the area in 1919 and River floods in 2014.

Causes:

- High rainfall in Winter of 2013/14 (peaked at 166mm in Jan 2014) saturated the soil.
- High tides in the Bristol Channel back up the rivers as they cannot drain quickly enough.
- Very flat landscape causes greater extent to flooding.
- Ditches hadn't been dredged since 1990's so had silted up reducing the capacity.

Effects:

- £20 million damage to residential property.
- £19 million pound cost to local government and rescue services.
- 4-week closure of railway cost the local economy £21 million and 80 roads closed cost £15 million.

Responses:

- Thirteen pumps bought in from Holland to pump out 7.3 million tonnes of water a day.
- Livestock removed to graze in other areas.
- The Government announced a £100 million scheme (medium term – up to 2020 & long term – up to 2035 aims).

Medium term

- Dredging operation on 2 rivers at a cost of £6 million.
- Embankments built around vulnerable villages (£180,000 to protect Thorney).
- Raising the height of the A372.

Long term

- Building a flood barrier at Bridgewater (£32 million) to reduce the impact of high tides stopping water escaping.
- Investigating a £16 million flood water storage scheme above Taunton to hold back water, including a large-scale tree planting scheme.

4.3 - Management of the River Severn at Shrewsbury

Location:

- Shrewsbury is the county town of Shropshire, UK and sits on the river Severn

Details:

- The Severn is the UKs longest river & a series of floods in 2000 prompted a management scheme to be built in Shrewsbury.
- £4.6 million scheme completed in 2004.
- Demountable (temporary) barriers used to hold back flood water when needed (held back 1.9m of floodwater in 2004).
- Land has been zoned so not all areas protected (low value playing fields and car parks are allowed to be flooded (reduces impacts further downstream).

4.4 - Landforms on the River Tees

Location:

- County Durham and North Yorkshire

Landforms:

- **Upper Course:** Water fall – High Force

- **Middle Course:** Meander - Barnard Castle

- **Lower Course:** Near Yarm – Oxbow Lakes and levees as well as Seal Sands estuary

*** you will be expected to explain how these features have been formed – not just naming examples ***

5. Case Studies - Coasts

5.1 - Storm Surge, December 2013

Location:

- Eastern coast of the UK

Causes:

- Deep depression (low pressure system) caused sea level to rise locally by 50cm.
- Strong winds created as a result of low pressure pushed the bulge of water towards land.
- High tides made the impacts worse along the East of England.
- Shape of the land funnelled the sea, further raising the height of the sea.

Effects

- 2 people were killed by high winds.
- 7 homes destroyed in Norfolk as cliff collapsed into the sea.
- In the Humber region 400 homes flooded.

Reponses

- 800,000 homes protected due to accurate forecasting & coastal defences in place.
- 1000 sandbags issued in Suffolk.
- Great Yarmouth – 9,000 homes evacuated as a precaution.
- Thames barrier was closed to protect London.

5.2 - Landforms on the Holderness Coastline

Location:

- East Coast of the UK - 61km from Flamborough in the north to Spurn Point in the south.

Landforms:

- **Flamborough:** Chalk cliff – erosion, features such as caves, arches and stacks, wave cut platforms.
- **Spurn point:** Around 3% of the material eroded from the Holderness Coast is deposited here each year.
- **Hornsea:** Sand and glacial till which is permeable overlays impermeable clay. This is prone to erosion by the coast as well as rotational slumping due to excess rain.

Impact of geology:

- Coastline is the fastest eroding stretch in Europe (now increased to 3m per year).
- At Hornsea, 100-year-old defences have been upgraded (New wave-return wall finished in 2003) as well as riprap and groynes used.
- Land-use reflects the defences used with a high-density urban area where defences in place and lower value farmland & caravan parks at both the North & South of the town.
- Mappleton however has not had any new sea defences and the old ones have fallen into disrepair.

5.3 - Landforms on the Dorset Coastline

Location:

- Jurassic coastline stretches from Exmouth in East Devon to Studland Bay in Dorset.
- World Heritage Site where coastal erosion has exposed a continuous sequence of rock formation covering Triassic, Jurassic and Cretaceous periods.

Landforms:

- Swanage - headland and bay.
- Durdle Door – sea arch
- Old Harry rocks (stack stump)
- Chesil Beach – bar

*** you will be expected to explain how these features have been formed – not just naming examples ***

5.4 - Managed Realignment - Medmerry scheme

Location:

- Medmerry, West Sussex, UK

Details:

- Moved a section of the coast 2km further in-land (example of 'retreating the line' in Shoreline management plans).
- Allowed an area to flood at high tide, reducing impacts elsewhere & absorbs the energy of the waves.
- A new 7km sea wall was built to protect the land behind.
- The scheme cost £28 million.

Successes:

- In 2014-15 it protected the coast effectively and was the first time that the Medmerry Holiday Village didn't have to deal with some flooding.
- Created new cattle grazing area (the fact they feed on saltmarsh gives a favour that is highly prized).
- New nature reserve was created which has increased tourism numbers.

Issues:

- Loss of productive farmland producing oilseed rape and winter wheat
- Built the same year as the Somerset Levels flooded so created conflict.

5.5 - Shoreline Management Plan - Borth

Location:

- Borth is a town in Wales that is built at the end of a spit, it is currently protected by Groynes but they have fallen into disrepair.

Details:

- Ceredigion Council used their SMP to split the coast into management units, Borth is 16.2.
- They decided against retreating the line (would affect homes behind the current defences) and advancing the line (no real need to).
- Decided to look at doing nothing (issues of erosion of the spit which would protect the important ecosystem of Borth Bog – a UNESCO site), homes and businesses would be flooded.
- Hold the line (Borth is valued at £10.75 million and defences will cost £7 million, new groynes would also starve sediment to Ynyslas which protects the whole estuary area).
- HOLD THE LINE was chosen with a new offshore reef to attract surfers as well as off-shore breakwaters (total cost £12 million).

5.6 - Thames Gateway scheme

Location:

- The Thames Estuary reaches from south-west London to where the river meets the North Sea, in the South East of Great Britain.

Details:

- The Thames estuary is a risk from storm surges like those in 1953 and 2013.
- Due to post-glacial rebound the area is sinking by 2mm a year.
- Climate change is causing se-level to rise by 3mm per year.
- Thames barrier was completed in 1982 & protects 1.25 million people from tidal floods.
- Barrier will not be effective if sea-levels rise by predicted 2.7m by 2100 (now created the TE2100 plan).

TE2100 plan
- Replace existing embankments.
- Increase inter-tidal habitat by 876 hectares (absorb flood water), created by managed realignment in Essex.
- Build a new longer barrier at Long Reach (would cost between £6 to £7 billion).

5.7 - Coastlines vulnerable to rising sea levels in the UK

Skegness (Lincolnshire)

- Poor road & rail links
- Highest concentration of static caravans in Europe (permanent homes for elderly and those on lower incomes)

Benbecula (Outer Hebrides)

- Population of only 1,200
- Economy in decline since 1970's since closure of military base
- Inefficient drainage system built in 1800
- Lack of jobs available for young people
- These are examples of poorer communities who may not be able to help themselves as sea-levels rise and communities & individuals are expected to protect themselves.

5.8 - Coastlines vulnerable to rising sea levels - Maldives

Location:

- The Maldives are a series of 1,190 islands in the Indian Ocean

Background:

- They have a population of 350,000, 1/3 of which lives in the capital city Malé.
- 80% of the land is less than 1m above sea-level (nowhere is more than 3m).
- GDP ranks it 165th out of 192 Nations (poorer country).

Potential impacts:

- Rise of 0.5m in sea-level by 2100 would see 77% underwater
- A rise of 1m would see the islands uninhabitable by 2085
- Japan has helped build a 3m sea wall (cost $60 Million) around Malé. All other islands remain vulnerable
- 87% of drinking water comes from collecting rainwater, groundwater supplies are being contaminated by rising sea water (salinisation)
- Tourism accounts for 90% of income (2004 tsunami affected beaches and saw a sharp decline in tourist number which have since recovered) which could be majorly impacted if beaches washed away.
- Australia has been expressed as a possible new home for the Maldivians if islands flooded (Australia may need to prepare for a wave of migrants)

Potential solutions:
- Dutch company has proposed a floating golf course that can be built off shore to provide for tourists as land dwindles.

6. Case Studies - Urbanisation

6.1 – Urbanisation in Mumbai

Location:

- Densely populated city on India's west coast.
- India's largest city.

Details:

- Dharavi Slum - 1 million people, 1 square mile, Largest slum in the world.
- Established slum in the centre (potters sector) and new-comers live in the edge of the slum.
- Only 1 toilet per 500 people.
- 85% employed.
- Over 15,000 factories but no regulation.
- Over 1 billion products are produced in the slum every year, but no tax is paid.
- Density within homes is very high.
- Little crime – cooperative community.
- 1 million bags of rubbish are collected every day in Mumbai.
- 80% of Mumbai rubbish is recycled in the slum.
- No division between religious groups.
- Toxic waste is next to the water pipes.
- Clean water only for 2 hours a day.
- Some property in the city is among the most expensive in the world.
- Previous redevelopment of slums into tower blocks has been unsuccessful.
- New redevelopment will mean only people who have lived in the slum since 2000 are eligible.
- No work space in the new tower blocks.

6.2 – Urbanisation in London

Location:

- South East of England
- Capital city of England and the UK

Background:

- London has always been a city of migrants – it has a very large London Irish Society and it even has the "London Welsh primary school" (Independent private school).
- There are over **300 languages spoken in London**, more than any other city in the world.
- Looking at the census for 2011, almost 45% are White British with the largest ethnic minority being 12% White Other (e.g. Europeans, Canadian's, American, Australian, New Zealand).

Why do people move to London?

- **Jobs** – jobs in London are well paid and there is a large range of them.
- **Education** – top universities as well as links to companies and NGO's, which encourage people to come and work for them after university.
- **Global industries** – such as financial services in Canary Wharf
- **Lifestyle** – there is a 24 hour industry in London which for many people is something very attractive for them.
- **Influences**

Regional	job, university, shopping / retail well established, ethnicity is well established, 24 hour services, sport – football, education
National	airports, sporting venues e.g. Wembley, education – top universities, Parliament / Government, Entertainment – West End, Historical sites, migration, influence of BBC
Global Context	airport (where most people land from overseas), financial capital in canary wharf & stock exchange, Royal family – commonwealth link, embassy's locations, tourism, influence of BBC

Impacts:

Social Impacts:	Ensuring that green spaces and historical buildings are preserved in new development
	More community services to try and bring people together
	It allows people to have their say in the development of where they live
	The regeneration of areas will include new housing and infrastructure for people
Environmental Impacts	Congestion charges to lower air and noise pollution
	The management of green areas that improve air quality
	Building regulations aim to lower any energy waste from houses
Economic Impacts	Tackling wage inequality between all people
	Ensuring more premises for new businesses and start ups
	Affordable housing needs to be provided for the growing population and this will hopefully help to reduce the poverty in many areas of London.

6.3 - Urbanisation in Leeds

Location:

- City in northern English county of Yorkshire

Background:

- Northern city with a population of over 850000.
- It has a large university population with 3 universities.
- Successful financial sector and wide transport links.

Employment:

- Leeds had the fastest growth in private sector jobs in 2016 compared to other UK cities.
- The financial sector is one of the biggest and is over 11% of total employment, with public sector the largest 18%.

Housing:

- Former industrial land is being redeveloped for student accommodation, restaurants and offices, such as Clarence Dock in 2007. However this was unsuccessful in 2012 when 28 of the 35 restaurant and retail units were empty. Rebranded in 2013 and called the New Dock with £250m investment.
- LILAC project – 20 sustainable houses built in Bramley, West Leeds. Housing is made of straw bale, has solar panels and operates a cooperative living. The project is Mutual Home Ownership Scheme and is priced so that it continues to allow families to live in the area.
- South Bank is a growing success - size to 350 football pitches, brownfield land, over 8000 new homes, preparation for HS2, improving opportunities in urban areas such as Hunslet.

Education:

- Leeds has a youthful population and growing numbers of English as an Additional Language pupils (EAL), especially in areas such as Armley, Beeston and Harehill.
- This increases the pressure on schools needing funding to support those pupils.

- In 2018 almost 300 primary and over 450 secondary pupils did not receive a school place, investment in new school places were by the council is over £4 million.

Waste:

- Fortnightly collection, food waste limited only to two areas and no plans to expand, which is a missed opportunity.

Transport:

- Sep 2018 - 1800 people from 176 organisations across West Yorkshire cycled nearly 270,000 miles during Cycle September.
- Participants saved almost 63,000 lbs of CO2 (cyclecityconnect.co.uk).
- New city centre loop, super cycle highway to encourage cycling safely (linking Bradford to Leeds though the west of the city – Armley, Pudsey and to the North Seacroft to Leeds city centre).

7. Case Studies - Development / Global issues

7.1 - Mali

Location:

- Sub-Saharan country of West Africa, which together with neighbouring countries are among some of the poorest in the world.
- It has no coastline (landlocked) and this makes it particularly difficult to move resources around.

Background:

- It has a population of around 18 million and is a former French colony.
- Vulnerable to natural disasters including a drought in 2005 and flooding in 2007.
- Over 60% of its population still lives in rural areas – many following traditionally nomadic lifestyle. It has a youthful population with over 40% under 15 years old.

Globalisation:

- Very few MNC operate in Mali – some are companies who have developed within the country e.g. Air Mali.
- Mali produces cotton, cereals and rice.
- Although locally produced rice now provides competition to imported Asian rice, Mali's primary export is cotton.
- Livestock exports and industry (producing vegetable and cottonseed oils, and textiles) have experienced growth.
- Although most of Mali is desert or semi-desert, the Niger River is a potential irrigation source.

Consequence of uneven development on Mali:

- Very unbalance between rural and urban – healthcare, water, education.
- Security – issues within the country / movement between.
- Kept poor – encouraged to "cash crops".

Reasons for MNC to locate in Mali:

- Not many but workforce / labour cheap due to youthful population.
- Linked to France / language.
- Rich in natural resources - Mali is now the 3rd largest gold mining country in Africa.

7.2 - Nike as MNC case study

Location:

- Headquarters are in the USA and sells and operates in over 140 countries.
- All its management operations and decisions (design, finance and marketing) are made in the USA.

Outsourcing:

- 41 countries manufacturing employing 48,000 directly worldwide.
- Manufacturing links in Vietnam, China, Indonesia, Sri Lanka, Thailand.
- Most garments made by women in textile factories.

Benefits for LIC – HOST COUNTRY

- Multiplier effect e.g. jobs created so local people have larger income and can spend money in shops, which in turn creates more jobs.
- Investment in infrastructure which can improve conditions for those in the local area (e.g. roads, water).
- Demand for housing increases which brings new services in the area.

Problems for LIC

- Workers have few rights including minimum wage or maximum hours.
- Government is too worried to put in laws like minimum wage as it might put companies off e.g. Thailand in 2013 introduce a minimum wage of US$10 and within 2 years the company had cut the number of jobs by a third.
- In Vietnam, the largest producer, many workers are migrants from rural areas.

Vietnam:

- Nike become its largest foreign employer with over 300,000 employed in 2015.
- But Nike made mistakes in the late 1990's.
- Subcontracted companies so all the profits went overseas, instead of staying in Vietnam.
- Factories gained reputation for poor sweatshop conditions.
- Vietnam Government attacked Nike for its practises – some were false but the harm was done. Nike told the Vietnamese government that if the attacks continued, they would leave – the government backed down.
- Nike did however improve some conditions in the factories, including working hours, wages and living accommodation.

7.3 - Aid projects

Location:

- Mali and Niger, West Africa.

Emergency aid:

- Food, shelter and medical supplies.

Long-term or development aid:

- Planned to tackle poverty, social and health issues (improving the quality of life).
- Examples of NGO's are Oxfam, Action Aid and Christian Aid.

Examples of Aid:

- UNICEF (United Nations International Children's Emergency Fund) is a charity that raises money for disasters and aid programmes.
- Promotion by World Health Organisation and UNICEF to improve maternal and child health – including supports 300 women's groups to promote breastfeeding, vaccination programs, vitamin supplements distributed.
- WaterAid - targeting slums in Mali's capital in order to prevent spread of waterborne diseases, access to water and sanitation.
- Christian Aid 2020 program to support the access to family planning and bring down the maternal mortality rate, fertility rate and the birth rate of Mali.

Fieldwork booklet

Key information

Geographical and numerical Skills

You will also need to be confident on a range of maths activities (these appear across all three papers). Most of these you will have studied in Maths and Science but it is important to practise them within your revision in Geography.

Fieldwork element:

This section covers all exam boards – the requirements are broadly the same. You will be examined on this with questions based on your own experiences of fieldwork and based on unseen elements.

You must do 2 days away from school site – one must have HUMAN features and the other much be PHYSICAL features. If you have missed one – speak to your teacher **URGENTLY**. You are will be examined on **BOTH**!

Focus for exam: EDUQAS only

This exam board requires certain tasks to be undertaken on the fieldwork. This would mean that there will be questions based on how you did the activities etc. below are the schedule of tasks:

2019	Geographical flows	Mitigating risk
2020	Qualitative surveys	Sustainable communities
2021	Change over time	Cycles and flows
2022	Qualitative surveys	Place

Focus for PEARSON / EDEXCEL A and B only

Candidates must do **one from two physical** environments (rivers or coasts) and **one from two human** environments (urban area or rural settlements).

Fieldwork Tips

This section of the specification is important to show the examiner that you can apply your understanding and have been outside of the classroom!!! It is important that you don't ignore it and not revise!

What you will need to remember:

- **Location** – be specific don't just say "Holderness coast".

- **Methods** – you will probably be asked about 2 – 3 but make sure you can describe all of them! You will need to say what you did to gather the information, why you did it, limitations of the methods.

- **Results** – you won't be expected to know every sites measurements or how many people answered yes on a questionnaire BUT you will need to take about the trends and it would benefit if you have some examples of data.

- **Data Presentation** – how did you show / present the results? What methods did you use to display them? Explain how and why you used these methods.

- **Conclusion** – simple – does it answer your hypothesis / aim! What do you learn!!! Be specific and link to results etc.

- **Evaluation** – you will need to be critical of your study – how could you improve it and why? What would this mean? What would be the limitations of it?

- **REPEAT** FOR BOTH HUMAN AND PHYSICAL

- **DON'T FORGET TO REVISE IT!!!**

How to: Analysis the results

Graphical

- You will need to write an analysis on the data presented to show that you have understood the results.
- Example:

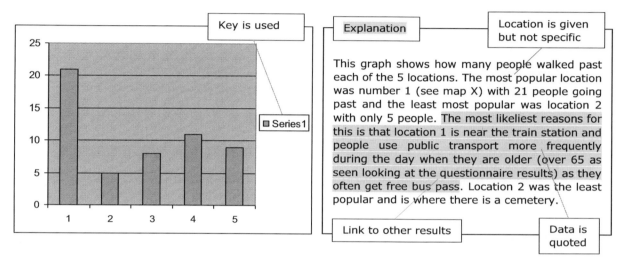

- When completing the analysis, you must:

    a) Quote data from the results
    b) Link to the graph / map
    c) Explain why they are like this e.g. *20 people out of 30 questioned on the day were over 65, this is because they are more likely not to work as they have reached the retirement age.*

Maps

- You will have used maps at some point during your fieldwork. This could be map that you have used to display your results and secondary maps such as OS Maps.

- When analysing a map, you should:

    - Use directions and grid references – e.g. South West, 415855
    - Look for anomalies and patterns and add some explanation e.g. *Traffic Flow map - showing "hotspots" of sites 2-4 where traffic is around the car park.*
    - Quote locations with detail such as footpath erosion - map and sites numbers with management

Photographs

- Use a key – e.g., number to show the examiner
- Look carefully to see what you can see e.g. double yellow lines, car park, traffic / pedestrian crossing.

Examples

- Read the below examples and assess the answers provided (note that these are real examples). What went well and how could they improve?

Example 1

- In our survey, local residents were asked whether tourism has had an impact on house prices, if they answered yes, they were then asked whether house prices have increased or decreased.

- **Question:** Describe and explain the impact that tourism has had on house prices.

- **Answer:** Yes, tourists had big impact one house pricing because tourists want to stay for longer so they buy the house and then the pricing for people who live there will increase

Example 2

- In our survey, tourists were asked the purpose of their visit.

- **Question:** Describe and explain the reasons for tourists visiting the area.

- **Answer:** The answer to this question shows clearly that 80% of the visitors are coming to the area for walking. This supports my findings with the footpath erosion rates and the fact we passed over 70 people walking on the footpath. Even in the town centre at lunch time, most people were wearing walking clothes so this shows that the national beauty of the area is the main draw for tourists.

	What went well	How could the answer be improved
Example 1		
Example 2		

Example 3

- **Question:** Compare three photographs of footpaths from our survey area. Annotate and explain the features observed.

- **Answer:**

Site 3	Site 4	Site 14
No real footpath, roots and very worn down.	Two paths formed as people have walked on their own and not behind each other	Near to Grassington. It has management

- It is clear that the paths are eroded by all the tourists. We saw 70 people on our visit. The paths near to Grassington have been managed.

Example 4

- **Question:** Describe these two photographs from our survey site and explain what they indicate about the area.

- **Answer:** These photos are shops in Masham, one is a sweet shop and the other is a clothing shop. They are a representation of the town's desirability and they show how it is well presented and is a reflection of how the whole town is presented. They are also a representation of the wide range and number of shops.

	What went well	How could the answer be improved
Example 3		
Example 4		

Geographical and Numerical Skills

The main skills that you will need to be confident in using:

Knowledge Checklist

Specification statement	Self-assessment		
	First review 4-7 months before exam	**Second review** 1-2 months before exam	**Final review** Week before exam
These are the bits the exam board wants you to know, make sure you can do all of these…			
I can use and calculate the median, mean, range.	☺ ☺ ☹	☺ ☺ ☹	☺ ☺ ☹
I can use and calculate quartiles and interquartile range, mode and modal class.	☺ ☺ ☹	☺ ☺ ☹	☺ ☺ ☹
I can label and annotate the features seen.	☺ ☺ ☹	☺ ☺ ☹	☺ ☺ ☹
I can interpret satellite images.	☺ ☺ ☹	☺ ☺ ☹	☺ ☺ ☹
I can use statistical sources such as census data to reach conclusions.	☺ ☺ ☹	☺ ☺ ☹	☺ ☺ ☹
I can use GIS to gather data.	☺ ☺ ☹	☺ ☺ ☹	☺ ☺ ☹
I can recognize different OS maps	☺ ☺ ☹	☺ ☺ ☹	☺ ☺ ☹
I can use 4-fig and 6 fig grid refences confidently.	☺ ☺ ☹	☺ ☺ ☹	☺ ☺ ☹
I can measure direct and indirect distance on a map.	☺ ☺ ☹	☺ ☺ ☹	☺ ☺ ☹
I can use a map to interpret relief.	☺ ☺ ☹	☺ ☺ ☹	☺ ☺ ☹
I can use alpha-numeric grid system	☺ ☺ ☹	☺ ☺ ☹	☺ ☺ ☹
I can use and create a flow map.	☺ ☺ ☹	☺ ☺ ☹	☺ ☺ ☹
I can create basic sketch map	☺ ☺ ☹	☺ ☺ ☹	☺ ☺ ☹
I can use and create desire line maps.	☺ ☺ ☹	☺ ☺ ☹	☺ ☺ ☹
I can use and create isoline maps.	☺ ☺ ☹	☺ ☺ ☹	☺ ☺ ☹

I can use and create desire line maps	☺ ☺ ☹	☺ ☺ ☹	☺ ☺ ☹
I can use and create proportional maps	☺ ☺ ☹	☺ ☺ ☹	☺ ☺ ☹
I can use an atlas index & contents page	☺ ☺ ☹	☺ ☺ ☹	☺ ☺ ☹
I can use latitude & longitude to locate places.	☺ ☺ ☹	☺ ☺ ☹	☺ ☺ ☹
I can use GOAD maps	☺ ☺ ☹	☺ ☺ ☹	☺ ☺ ☹
I can use a choropleth map	☺ ☺ ☹	☺ ☺ ☹	☺ ☺ ☹
I can use and create bar charts	☺ ☺ ☹	☺ ☺ ☹	☺ ☺ ☹
I can use and create line graphs	☺ ☺ ☹	☺ ☺ ☹	☺ ☺ ☹
I can use and create pie charts	☺ ☺ ☹	☺ ☺ ☹	☺ ☺ ☹
I can use and create scatter graph	☺ ☺ ☹	☺ ☺ ☹	☺ ☺ ☹
I can use and create divergent bar	☺ ☺ ☹	☺ ☺ ☹	☺ ☺ ☹
I can use and create divergent line	☺ ☺ ☹	☺ ☺ ☹	☺ ☺ ☹
I can use and create compound bar	☺ ☺ ☹	☺ ☺ ☹	☺ ☺ ☹
I can use and create compound line	☺ ☺ ☹	☺ ☺ ☹	☺ ☺ ☹
I can use and create triangle graphs	☺ ☺ ☹	☺ ☺ ☹	☺ ☺ ☹
I can use and create radial diagram	☺ ☺ ☹	☺ ☺ ☹	☺ ☺ ☹
I can use and create logarithmic scale	☺ ☺ ☹	☺ ☺ ☹	☺ ☺ ☹
I can use and create dispersion diagrams	☺ ☺ ☹	☺ ☺ ☹	☺ ☺ ☹

Practice Questions

1. Here is the temperature of one location over 45 years. Use this data to answer the questions:

1970	1975	1980	1985	1990	1995	2000	2005	2010	2015
3 °C	8 °C	3 °C	2 °C	1 °C	0 °C	0 °C	1 °C	1 °C	2 °rc

a) What is the range of this data?

....
....

b) Calculate the mean.

....
....

c) Suggest the trends of the temperature at this location.

....
....

2. Complete the pie chart below with the missing data and key:

In B&B/ Hotel	Camping	Staying with friends/ family	Other
30	0	5	15

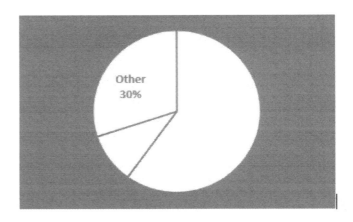

3. The results of the river fieldwork looking at the size of pebbles is shown in the table below.

Sample	Pebble size in centimetres
1	15
2	8
3	7
4	9
5	11
6	4
7	12
8	10
9	6
10	12
11	21

a) What is the range of the data?

....

b) Calculate the interquartile range of the pebble size data. Show your working in the space below

....

c) Suggest how you could display this information and justify your reasons.

....
....
....
....
....

4. Using the grid below, give the 4 figure and 6 figure coordinates.

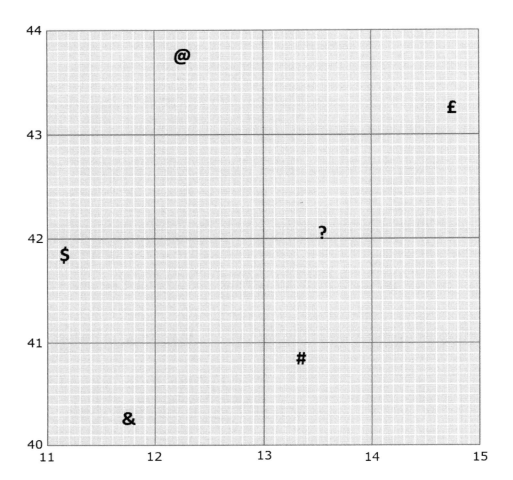

- 4 Figure
  a. £ .... b. $ .... c. ? ....
  d. @ .... e. # .... f. & ....

- 6 Figure
  a. £ .... b. $ .... c. ? ....
  d. @ .... e. # .... f. & ....

Fieldwork

Knowledge Checklist

Specification statement These are the bits the exam board wants you to know, make sure you can do all of these...	Self-assessment		
	First review 4-7 months before exam	**Second review** 1-2 months before exam	**Final review** Week before exam
I can describe how to prepare for a fieldwork trip with use of Risk Assessment.	☺ ☺ ☹	☺ ☺ ☹	☺ ☺ ☹
I can describe how to create hypothesis based on a theme.	☺ ☺ ☹	☺ ☺ ☹	☺ ☺ ☹
I can explain how to structure an induction and what to include.	☺ ☺ ☹	☺ ☺ ☹	☺ ☺ ☹
I can explain the methods of PRIMARY data collection used.	☺ ☺ ☹	☺ ☺ ☹	☺ ☺ ☹
I can explain the methods of SECONDARY data collection used.	☺ ☺ ☹	☺ ☺ ☹	☺ ☺ ☹
I can describe the methods of data presentation used.	☺ ☺ ☹	☺ ☺ ☹	☺ ☺ ☹
I can explain why the methods of data presentation was the most suitable.	☺ ☺ ☹	☺ ☺ ☹	☺ ☺ ☹
I can write a conclusion using data from a fieldwork.	☺ ☺ ☹	☺ ☺ ☹	☺ ☺ ☹
I can evaluation on fieldwork.	☺ ☺ ☹	☺ ☺ ☹	☺ ☺ ☹
Unseen fieldwork			
I can create a hypothesis using photographs and background information.	☺ ☺ ☹	☺ ☺ ☹	☺ ☺ ☹
I can risk assess using the photographs to ensure it is safe.	☺ ☺ ☹	☺ ☺ ☹	☺ ☺ ☹
I can describe and explain the appropriate primary methods	☺ ☺ ☹	☺ ☺ ☹	☺ ☺ ☹
I can describe and explain the methods of SECONDARY data collection used.	☺ ☺ ☹	☺ ☺ ☹	☺ ☺ ☹
I can describe the methods of data presentation used.	☺ ☺ ☹	☺ ☺ ☹	☺ ☺ ☹
I can explain which methods of data presentation are the most suitable.	☺ ☺ ☹	☺ ☺ ☹	☺ ☺ ☹
I can suggest a conclusion using data from a fieldwork.	☺ ☺ ☹	☺ ☺ ☹	☺ ☺ ☹
I can evaluation the fieldwork.	☺ ☺ ☹	☺ ☺ ☹	☺ ☺ ☹

Your HUMAN fieldwork

- Complete these activities to keep a neat summary

Location:

What was the aim of your fieldwork?

Hypothesis:

....

....

Minor Hypothesis:

....

....

Methods

Name the methods of data collection that you undertook with a brief description:

Primary Methods:

....

....

....

....

....

....

....

....

....

....

....

Secondary Methods:

....

....

....

....

....

....

....

....

....

Data Presentation

Name the main methods of data presentation that you did and give a summary of how you did it (e.g. I created proportional arrows by ….)

....
....
....
....
....
....
....
....
....
....
....
....
....
....
....
....

Analysis and Conclusion

What did you find out? How does it help you prove / disprove the aim? Link to theory to support conclusion can also be useful.

....
....
....
....
....
....
....
....
....
....
....
....
....
....
....

Practice Questions

1. Explain which primary method was the most successful in collecting enough data.

....
....
....
....
....
....
....
....

2. Explain which method was the most difficult to collect.

....
....
....
....
....
....
....
....

3. Describe one method in detail, step by step.

....
....
....
....
....
....
....
....

4. Suggest how you could improve the methods used.

    ....
    ....
    ....
    ....
    ....
    ....
    ....
    ....
    ....

5. Explain the HUMAN aspect that you focused on.

    ....
    ....
    ....
    ....
    ....
    ....
    ....
    ....

6. Using your data presentation methods, assess the results show and link it to your aim.

    ....
    ....
    ....
    ....
    ....
    ....
    ....
    ....

7. Evaluate the reliability of your data presentation.

....
....
....
....
....
....
....
....

8. Suggest one other data presentation method that could have been used and explain why.

....
....
....
....
....
....
....
....

9. Summaries the main findings of your fieldwork.

....
....
....
....
....
....
....
....

10. Evaluate the usefulness of your fieldwork.

....
....
....
....
....
....
....
....

Your PHYSICAL fieldwork

- Complete these activities to keep a neat summary

Location:

What was the aim of your fieldwork?

Hypothesis:

....

....

Minor Hypothesis:

....

....

Methods

Name the methods of data collection that you undertook with a brief description:

Primary Methods:

....

....

....

....

....

....

....

....

....

....

....

Secondary Methods:

....

....

....

....

....

....

....

....

Data Presentation

Name the main methods of data presentation that you did and give a summary of how you did it (e.g. I created proportional arrows by ....)

....
....
....
....
....
....
....
....
....
....
....
....
....
....
....
....

Analysis and Conclusion

What did you find out? How does it help you prove / disprove the aim? Link to theory to support conclusion can also be useful.

....
....
....
....
....
....
....
....
....
....
....
....
....
....
....

Practice Questions

1. Suggest two reasons why undertaking a risk assessment is vital for planning a fieldwork.

....
....
....
....
....
....
....
....

2. Assess suitability of your location.

....
....
....
....
....
....
....
....

3. Describe how you collected one secondary method.

....
....
....
....
....
....
....
....

4. Explain which secondary method was the least successful.

....
....
....
....
....
....
....
....

5. Explain which primary method was the most difficult to collect.

....
....
....
....
....
....
....
....

6. Suggest how you could improve one method used.

....
....
....
....
....
....
....
....

7. Explain what PHYSICAL aspect that you focused on.

....
....
....
....
....
....
....
....

8. Using one data presentation, evaluate the reliability of your data.

....
....
....
....
....
....
....
....

9. Summarize the main findings of your fieldwork.

....
....
....
....
....
....
....
....

10. Evaluate the usefulness of your fieldwork.

....
....
....
....
....
....
....
....

Unseen fieldwork example #1

Practice exam-style questions:

1. Suggest the usefulness of geographical theory (background) in planning your fieldwork.

   ....
   ....
   ....
   ....
   ....
   ....
   ....
   ....

2. Explain the purpose of setting aims / hypothesis.

   ....
   ....
   ....
   ....
   ....
   ....
   ....
   ....

3. Identify whether these are primary or secondary methods of data collection and the write a brief description of how you would collect the data.

	Primary	Secondary	Describe how you would collect data using this method
Transect			
GIS			
Pedestrian count			
Traffic count			
Maps e.g. Bing, OS			
Bi-polar or Environmental Quality Survey			
Groin height method			
Historical data			

4. What does the phrase "data presentation" mean?

....

....

....

....

....

....

....

....

5. What is the difference between a closed question and an open questionnaire? Suggest a reason why one would be the most useful type to use.

....
....
....
....
....
....
....
....

6. Using the data below, decide which type of data presentation is the most suitable and explain why.

How did you travel here today?

Bus / Coach	4
Car	30
Walk	4
Motorbike	20
Other	0

....
....
....
....
....
....

7. Using the photograph below, answer the questions:

a)

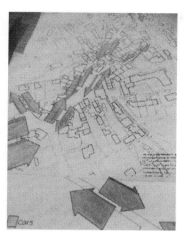

Name the method.

....

Suggest what data would be suitable to use this method.

....

Describe the method used.

....
....
....
....

Explain the reasons for using this method.

....
....
....
....

Suggest an alternative method of presenting this data.

....
....

b)

Name the method.

....

Suggest what data would be suitable to use this method.

....

Describe the method used.

....
....
....
....

Explain the reasons for using this method.

....
....
....
....

Suggest an alternative method of presenting this data.

....
....

8. Give one advantage and one disadvantage of this method of data presentation.

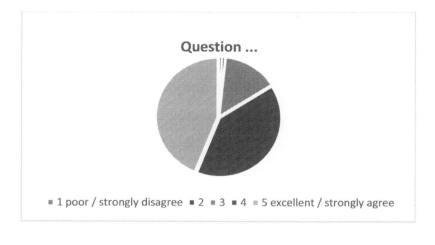

....

....

....

....

....

....

9. Analyse the following graph, based on different fieldwork approaches.

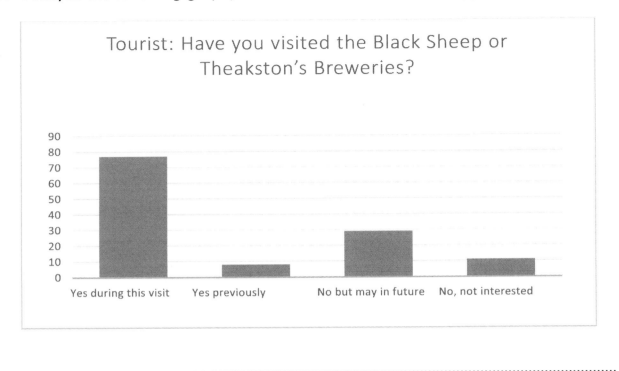

Tourist: Have you visited the Black Sheep or Theakston's Breweries?

....
....
....
....
....
....
....
....
....
....
....
....
....
....
....
....
....
....
....
....
....
....
....

10. Explain the differences between qualitative and quantitative data. Use at least on example for each.

....
....
....
....
....
....
....
....
....
....

11. What was the method that you used to collect / conduct a flow?

....
....
....
....

a) What were the limitations of this method?

....
....
....
....

b) Suggest **two** ways that you could make your use of flow more reliable.

....
....
....
....

12. Suggest how you could investigate sustainability within a physical environment.

....
....
....
....
....
....
....
....

Specific topic fieldwork questions

- Some of these might not be relevant to your exam board specification, however may still be useful.

Coastal

1. Explain how the rate of coastal erosion can be measured using secondary data.

....
....
....
....

2. Explain why house prices are likely to be higher in areas with multiple coastal defences.

....
....
....
....

3. Describe how you could investigate whether the sea defences appear to be adequate / well maintained at a location (e.g. Hornsea).

....
....
....
....
....
....
....
....

4. Suggest which data collection methods you would use. Explain your reasons why.

....
....
....
....
....
....
....
....

River

1. Describe how you would investigate the vulnerability of a town from flooding

....
....
....
....
....
....
....
....

2. Suggest how you would investigate the success of river defences.

....
....
....
....
....
....
....
....

3. Describe how you would investigate to see if the Bradshaw model (or other geographical theory) applied to a river.

....
....
....
....
....
....
....
....

4. Evaluate the usefulness of the environment agencies flood map planning and / or other GIS within planning of a fieldwork.

....
....
....
....
....
....
....
....

Urban environment

1. Describe how you would investigate to see what the land use pattern of your chosen location.

....
....
....
....
....
....
....
....

2. Discuss how you can use secondary data to display data (e.g. CCTV)

....
....
....
....
....
....
....
....

3. Suggest how you would investigate the change of demographic in an urban area.

....
....
....
....
....
....
....
....

4. Evaluate the usefulness of the census as secondary data.

....
....
....
....
....
....
....
....

Rural environment

1. Discuss how pedestrian counts at different times can be useful in showing the impact of tourism.

    ....
    ....
    ....
    ....
    ....
    ....
    ....
    ....

2. Suggest which methods of data collection would be useful in investigating the impact of tourism.

    ....
    ....
    ....
    ....
    ....
    ....
    ....
    ....

3. Discuss the limitation of 2 methods of data collection.

    ....
    ....
    ....
    ....

4. Evaluate the usefulness of secondary sources such as trip advisor.

    ....
    ....
    ....
    ....
    ....
    ....
    ....

Unseen fieldwork example #2

- This section is a core element. You will be given resources and need to use your knowledge to apply what you've experienced on your own fieldwork

Background

- GCSE students are visiting a honeypot in the Yorkshire Dales.
- The first part of their study is a 2 mile walk along a footpath between Hebden and Grassington.
- The second part relates to time within the village of Grassington.
- They will be assessing "How and why is the impact of tourism being managed in Grassington?"

Part 1:

- Using the images and your own understanding of issues within rural areas, complete the questions below:

1. Create a hypothesis or aim to investigate the area and the issues seen in the photographs.

   ....
   ....
   ....
   ....
   ....
   ....
   ....
   ....

2. Explain the advantages of the location shown above for creating a fieldwork enquiry.

   ....
   ....
   ....
   ....
   ....
   ....
   ....
   ....

3. Describe 2 primary data collection methods that would be appropriate to gather information on your hypothesis. Explain your reasons why.

   ....
   ....
   ....
   ....
   ....
   ....
   ....
   ....

4. Suggest a secondary data collection method that would support your aim.

....
....
....
....
....
....
....
....

5. Identify 2 possible hazards and create a risk assessment based on this.

....
....
....
....
....
....
....
....

6. Suggest the possible reasons for footpath management as seen in photograph E.

....
....
....
....
....
....
....
....

7. Using graph below, evaluate the usefulness of the data presentation seen.

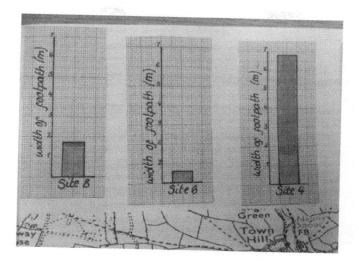

....
....
....
....
....
....
....
....
....

8. Returning in 12 months is one possible method of gathering further data. Suggest advantages and disadvantages to this.

....
....
....
....
....
....
....
....

Part 2:

- The students continue their fieldwork into Grassington village.
- They investigate the following hypothesis:

"Due to its rural location and visitor attractions such as the Folk Museum, Grassington will have a large sphere of influence of the town of its size.
"

- Using the images below, answer the following questions.

9. Using the images, identify 2 issues that could be occurring in the town.

....
....
....
....

10. Suggest 2 methods of collecting data that students could take part to look to look at the number of visitors in the area. Explain your choices.

....

....

....

....

....

....

....

11. Suggest the three groups of people that might be targeted for a questionnaire. Explain the reasons why.

....

....

....

....

....

....

....

....

12. Complete the bi-polar / Environmental Quality Survey.

	5	4	3	2	1	
Attractive location						Unattractive location
No Litter						Lots of litter
Few pedestrians						Overcrowded

13. Using the example below of presenting the EQS / Bipolar results, suggest the limitations of this method. (*HINT*: use of a 0 axis and a negative score)

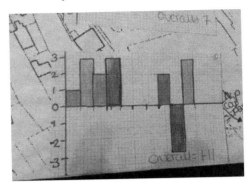

....
....
....
....
....
....
....
....

14. Students have attempted to write up the results from their study. Studying the two examples, annotate positive aspects as well as areas to improve on in their write up:

A	Site 1 was near the center of Grassington. It scored low (-2 and -3) for traffic and lots of street furniture but that was to be expected. There was some greenery and this was scored at +1 as a result. The overall result for this site was -6 and the environment is clearly affected by tourism.
B	Using the EQS results I noticed that sites that scored better (+1-+3) were further from the town center. These had higher scores on little traffic and greenery. However, they often had less few locations with street furniture (unlike site 1 and 3 which was -3) however these were clearly more residential than site 1 and 3 which were in the town and more tourist areas.

....
....
....
....

15. Evaluate the proposed fieldwork and whether it will achieve its aims.

....
....
....
....
....
....
....
....

Model Fieldwork Summary

- Create your own notes based on your fieldworks however you could use this as a useful tool as part of revision.

Location

- Hornsea – seaside town on the east coast of the UK
- Grassington – North Yorkshire town within the national park

Risk Assessment

- Identify the risks and then say how we can limit them to stop them being a problem:
    - Weather
    - Footpath (trip along the path etc)
    - River (Grassington only)
    - Sea (Hornsea only)
    - Public
    - Transport

Methods of data collection

- Primary – ones we collect ourselves:

    - Transect (Used for making notes and taking photographs in Hornsea, for looking at the width of the footpath in Grassington and how deep the path was).
    - Questionnaires – local and tourist.
    - Traffic Count – 20 minutes in AM and 20 min PM.
    - Pedestrian Count - 20 minutes in AM and 20 min PM.
    - Bipolar survey (-3 to +3 scoring of sites).

- Secondary – information we gather from other sources:

    - Trip Advisor reviews – Sphere of influence.
    - Maps – travel routes and times, areas to avoid due to access.

Limitations:

- These are things that make the method less than reliable:

    - Only collecting on one day / time = better if you can revise on a weekend to see the difference in the number of people.
    - Bipolar = based on your opinion to each location at that time only – could change if weather / litter / how busy etc.
    - Trip Advisor = only based on those who fill in the reviews and if they post their accurate location. Some locations are broad e.g. county wide and others are smaller area.

Data presentation

Data	Method	How to do it	Issue / limitation
Questionnaire	Pie charts and bar graphs	Using excel	Multiple choice questions used to help make it easier to analysis but can force "best fit" answer
Transect of footpath	Photograph and mini graph	Large map with photographs for each site and then a graph to show the erosion of the site – below 1.5m green above 1.5m red (1.5 m is the national park limit).	Graphs might not show the whole area of erosion.
Traffic count	Propitiated arrows	Work out 1mm to 2 vehicles Right and Left arrow on map to show the flow	Difficult to see on map when sites are near each other.
Pedestrian count	Isopleth	Data into 3 categories and then colour code with the highest in the darkest colour.	Big range of data so can make it look like a different pattern.

Data Analysis

- Look for trends / patterns – did all the locations far away from the town centre have fewer people? Why might that be?
- Does all the evidence show the same or is there some that show something different? Why do you think this?
- How can it relate to the wider topic / issue?

Conclusion

- Linking back to the hypothesis and saying whether true or false and why you think that (linking to the evidence found).

Evaluation

- How you can make your study better and why:

    - Return on a weekend in the summer because … it will be busier so you can see how much of the area is affected etc
    - Use further secondary data e.g. different review websites, national park own data on the area, museum data on where people come from.
    - Was the information accuracy, reliability and bias? Why? What would you do to tackle this?

Answers

- These answers should be used as a prompt - there are many different possibilities. Use your own lessons and case studies to form your extended answers. You need to understand the content and know it well before working on your technique.

- **You will need to look at the marks awarded per question to understand how to structure the answers.**

- Point mark:

Mark	Type of question	How marks awarded
2	Definition	Must be correct – could have some red herrings (so look for slight errors)
3	Gap fill / complete	Correct term / feature example needs to be given.
2	Describe from a source such as graph	Point mark but be cautious that you use it correctly as some might require you to give data from the source e.g. *temperature risks by 3 °C between Jan and March.*
4	List	

- Level mark: **(Look at these carefully!)**

Mark	Type of question	How marks awarded
4	Reason / compare	2 tiers (excluding 0) p33 https://www.eduqas.co.uk/qualifications/geography/gcse-b/GCSE-Geog-B-SAMs.pdf
6	Discuss / Explain	3 tiers (excluding 0) p32 https://www.eduqas.co.uk/qualifications/geography/gcse-b/GCSE-Geog-B-SAMs.pdf
8	Give / Explain / justify Support the statement	4 tiers (excluding 0) p34 https://www.eduqas.co.uk/qualifications/geography/gcse-b/GCSE-Geog-B-SAMs.pdf
SPAG		Level 3 tiers (excluding 0) p35 https://www.eduqas.co.uk/qualifications/geography/gcse-b/GCSE-Geog-B-SAMs.pdf

Exam command words:

Analyze	You need to look at data / source etc. and weigh up what the information is telling you and reach a conclusion.
Annotate	This is more than labelling – you need to give depth like reasons / explanations / used key terms.
Assess / Discuss / Evaluate	You need to weigh up the issues and the strategies used to see which one is the best / most effective. You will need to use examples to support points.
Complete	You need to complete part of the question – it could be a gap fill, graph, or diagram. Be careful that you don't miss these out and make sure it also makes sense (e.g. sentence reads accurately).
Create / Draw	Here you need to draw or create something – could be one diagram or a series of diagrams.
Demonstrate	This is where you need to show something – will probably have a second command word that you will need to use.
Describe	This is where you just say what it is – what the process is not why it happens.
Explain	You need to say why something happens – the reasons for it and would need detail.

Revision workbook answers

THEME 1: CHANGING PLACES – CHANGING ECONOMIES

KEY IDEA 1.1: Urbanization in contrasting global cities

1. Define the following terms:
   a. global city and megacity
   b. Explain the differences between them.

   Global city = city connected with worldwide, interconnected and influential – e.g. Milan for fashion. Mega City = city with more than 10 million.

2. Describe the distribution of global cities around the world and the link between them and mega cities.

   Distribution is about the spread of cities. Global cities are often connected from historic links e.g. New York, Milan, London and mostly in HIC. Mega cities are not always a direct link as many global cities in HIC are not mega cities or just reach that criteria (e.g. London). Mega cities are mostly in newly industrialised countries e.g. Brazil, India, China. Growing cities are now being seen in low income countries (LIC) such as Uganda.

3. Explain the main reasons for growth within urban areas in HIC.
   - Opportunities for high income professional jobs tend to be only seen in urban areas (e.g. cities such as Manchester and Leeds have seen huge growth).
   - Transport links – access to wide range of transport e.g. airport, tram, train.
   - Highly educated workforce remaining in university cities after completing university

4. Explain the main reasons for the growth within urban areas in developing countries.
   - High natural population growth from having youthful population (not necessity people having large number of babies).
   - access to employment compared to rural areas
   - access to health care and education
   - rural to urban pull

5. Using your chosen location, describe the social, economic and cultural patterns within the area.

   This needs to be very clear – you must make sure that your location is appropriate, remember you will have studied two cities – one in HIC cities and the second either a LIC or newly industrialized country (NIC), so pick the city that works for this question – do not do both!

e.g. Mumbai, India
Social: multicultural and religion – Dharavi population co-exists with different faiths.
Economic: The slum generates at least $650 million per year, 85% of people have a job in the slum and work within the community, small businesses – often only employing one or two people.
Cultural: strong communities within the Dharavi potters area of the slum, cooperative and shared living space, language remains from the rural areas that the potters came from (Gujarat).

6. Describe how urban developments have changed in the UK over time.

Focus on your area carefully – you could use your HIC city if it's a UK based one to reduce learning more case studies.

Leeds Case Study:

Former industrial land being redeveloped for student accommodation, restaurants and offices such as Clarence Dock 2007 however it was unsuccessful in 2012 when 28 of the 35 restaurant and retail units were empty. Rebranded in 2013 and called the New Dock with £250m investment.

South Bank growing success - size to 350 football pitches, brownfield land, over 8000 new homes, preparation for HS2, improving opportunities in urban areas such as Hunslet.

7. Give 3 impacts of urbanisation on both your locations.
   * House prices increased, making it more unaffordable for lower income.
   * Transport increasing leading to more pollution – investment is happening with the redevelopment including HS2 planning, park and ride extended in Elland Road, extension of the cycle highway.
   * New city centre park – to support the aim to improve the environment.

8. Explain the problems in your locations have with poverty and deprivation.
   Look at the evidence and name food banks. Give some crime and homelessness statistics to develop depth in your answer,

   e.g. The West Leeds food bank has struggled with the increase in demand since 2013....

9. Explain how infrastructure (roads), transport and waste disposal have impacts on your urban area and how it is being resolved.
   New city centre loop, super cycle highway to encourage cycling safely (linking Bradford to Leeds though the west of the city – Armley, Pudsey and to the North Seacroft to Leeds city centre).

Sep 2018: 1800 people from 176 organisations across West Yorkshire cycled nearly 270,000 miles during Cycle September. Participants saved almost 63,000 lbs of CO_2 (cyclecityconnect.co.uk)

Waste – fortnightly collection, food waste only to two limited areas and no plans to expand = missed opportunity.

10. Analysis the strategies which aim to reduce inequality and improve the lives of people living within developing urban areas.

Consider issues: Education, housing, transport and employment. Which strategies have helped – cycle routes help people commute of cheaper and healthier, housing redeveloped improves the quality of housing but can increase the cost. Employment – is it employment for all or just certain groups.

KEY IDEA: 1.2 Urban and rural processes and change in the UK

1. Define the following terms:
   a. counter-urbanisation

      movement from urban areas to rural areas

   b. brownfield

      sites that have already been built on

   c. greenfield

      sites that have never been built on

2. Explain the advantages and disadvantages of redevelopment and development has on both greenfield and brownfield sites.
   - <u>Adv brownfield:</u> often have services already there including water which brings down the cost of redevelopment.
   - <u>Disadv brownfield:</u> cost of decontaminating land from former industrial background.
   - <u>Adv greenfield:</u> not been shaped by previous developments so fresh start.
   - <u>Disadv greenfield:</u> local people don't often support the plans.

3. Using London as an example, explain why it has a housing shortage and the impacts this has.

   High population growth in all sectors, lack of social housing being built, overcrowded housing, transport links making commuting difficult to some areas, government policies on investment favours London. **Impact-**

housing costs so high that overcrowded housing of poor quality is often the only option for low income families.

4. Describe how rural areas in the UK are changing.
   - Think carefully about change and make sure you focus on the rural areas. E.g. ageing population as younger move to cities, house prices increasing due to counter urbanisation, congestion increases with new builds. Greenfield land being built on.
   - DON'T EXPLAIN!!!

5. Give main features of high street and out-of-town retail locations and explain at least two of them.
   - High Street – mixture of shops with a range of sizes of units, often in decline e.g. boarded up shops, lack of access to parking, EXPLAIN – lack of parking restricts the accessibility of the shops for key groups of people e.g. elderly resulting in the grey pound being spent elsewhere.
   - Out of town – often with clear and easy car access (without other transport links), most shops / units filled, big brands rather than independent (due to rent costs).

6. Define the following terms and explain how this is changing retail.
   a. high street
      traditional shopping areas, mixed experiences, empty units, access of other transport methods, independent shops returning with rent reductions

   b. out of town shopping
      retail parks based on the outskirts of the city / town - ease of parking, dominated by big brands

   c. mobile shopping
      shopping on apps – increasing since 2010, quick payment so people don't need to input their card details

   d. internet shopping
      continuous growth over the last 15 years, consumers like the ease of comparing prices, buying multiple items to try on at home (very popular)

7. Define the term honeypot and give examples of issues within these areas.
   - Honeypot – attractive area that has high tourism that can put pressure on the environment and society and resulting with negatively impacts.
   - Issues – traffic causing congestion, house prices increasing with second home ownership, litter, footpath erosion.

8. Evaluate the effectiveness of strategies to manage a place that is under pressure from too many visitors.

> Grassington Yorkshire Dales – double yellow lines, national park car park for a small fee, 10% are second homes in the wider area – calls for increase in council tax to stop second homes (https://www.theguardian.com/money/2017/dec/03/yorkshire-dales-councils-plan-tax-crackdown-on-second-home-owners)

9. Create a table with the positive and negative impacts of major sporting event (e.g. Olympics, Tour de Yorkshire).

> Depends on your case study – you need to have figures but consider e.g. congestion from the visitor numbers, parking (negative is pressure but positive is income for the council etc.), accommodation (revenue but also makes it difficult if regular as it pushes up prices), environmental impacts (parking on verges, footpaths eroded, litter), building work (facilities, accommodation – is it left empty?).

10. Define the term sustainable community and using an example, explain how a sustainable community operates.

> Sustainable communities – communities that try to reduce their impact on the environment and allow the community to continue develop e.g. sustainable transport with cycle lanes, allotments, energy, housing – each reduces the impact on the environment but also makes the community work together. Bedzed London is a great example.

KEY IDEA: 1.3 A global perspective on development issues

1. Describe three different indicators of development.
   - Birth rate – number of live births per 1000 of the population.
   - Fertility rate – number of babies expected to be born to a woman on average. Lower the number indicates higher rates of education a woman has.
   - Life expectancy at birth – this shows how old a baby born is expect to live to – useful to indicate the level of medical care.

2. Explain why trade, technology, industry and migration help to create stronger links between countries.
   - Make sure you understand the terms.
   - Link between – trade of primary products leads to dependency, increased migration from the country with primary resources to the one that is manufacturing / developing the technology etc. Reliance between countries creates strong relationships in multiple areas and industries.

3. Define the term: MNC and give two examples.

   MNC – multinational cooperation's – countries based in multiple countries, often with head quarter in high income countries and manufacturing in a low-income country where the costs of production are lower. E.g. Coca-Cola, Apple

4. Explain the reasons for the emergence of NICs.

   NIC – newly industrial countries e.g. Indonesia

   Reasons – costs of labour are lower which increases the profit, lower health & safety and environmental laws which reduces the costs of manufacturing.

5. Explain the benefits and disadvantages of MNC investment on the environment, economy and society in one region/country.

   - <u>Benefits:</u> environment – often has some improvements in flood defences, economy – increased jobs and therefore wages and taxes, society – education and skills improve in order to create the jobs.
   - <u>Disadvantages:</u> environment – pollution increases as companies use cheap methods to remove wages, economy – remission of profit form income, society – migration increases putting pressure on housing, education etc.

6. Define what fair trade is and explain the benefits.

   - Fair trade – trade where farmers are paid a reasonable price for their produce.
   - Farmers have a higher income which means they can reinvest in their own farms and families, including education for their children and environment pressures can be reduced as farmers are under less pressure to produce higher yields.

7. Explain the positive and negative consequences of development in one NIC.

   <u>NIC: India</u>
   - <u>Positive:</u> higher skills and education as secondary industries are established, income increases leading to multiplier effects.
   - <u>Negative:</u> higher migration to urban areas, environmental issues such as waste.

8. Define the following terms tariffs/ trade blocs/ quotas.

   - Tariffs: tax on product – often used to make it imports less favourable than home produce.
   - Trade blocs: agreement between countries regarding the trading products by promoting trade between each other.
   - Quotas: fixed number of a particular product

9. Explain how the structure of trade (e.g. tariffs/ trade blocs/ quotas etc) impacts on patterns of global development.

Favours one country or trade bloc over another that can result in the changes of pricing, promotes migration between the counties linked in trading blocs, quotas can restrict the access and availability of products.

10. Assess the development priorities for one NIC where long-term development aid is needed.

Long term aid focuses on development such as clean water, education and healthcare provision. These focuses (use your own case study) allow for more long-term sustainable development within your NIC. Look at the successes of the aid and whether it has successes in development e.g. *education rates increased in X including ...*

THEME 2: CHANGING ENVIRONMENTS

KEY IDEA 2.1: Shaping the landscape - coasts and coastal management

1) Define the following terms:
   a. Geology

   The study of the soil and rocks and how it influences landscapes

   b. Erosion

   Breakdown of landforms / material by water (rain, sea), wind

   c. Retreat

   Moving backwards of the coastline from erosion

2) Explain how erosion breaks down material.

   When there is a crack in rock, water (and wind) exploit that crack and can get in. Once in this gap it weakens the surrounding rock causing it to become unstable which eventually means it will collapse.

3) Describe how resistant rock (hard) forms a headland.

   Resistant rock is harder and therefore less likely to become weakened by erosion. The softer rock is targeted first, meaning it will become vulnerable and become eroded. This creates landforms whereby the weakened areas (both resistant and soft rock). Landforms along a headland include arches, stacks, stumps, coves, beaches.
   ** being able to draw and annotate is useful

4) Draw and annotate a diagram of a spit.

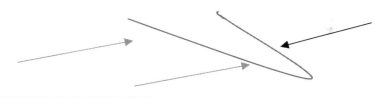

Spit is made up of sand and shingle. It is vulnerable to changes from storms etc. and can be washed away quickly.

Prevailing wind – long shore drift occurring

Forms together with shallow sea bed, changing coastal landscape

5) Name and describe the transportation methods.

Longshore drift – movement of sand and other beach material from one place to another. It occurs due to prevailing wind (strongest wind) that hits the beach at an angle. Each set of waves deposits material with the swash and takes material back to the sea (at a straighter angle due to the gravity of the moon) in the backwash. This results in material being moved along the shoreline.

6) Name 3 methods of hard engineering and explain how each works.

- **Sea Wall** – two types curved (modern) and straight. Wall build at the end of the coastline where a promenade is often formed to take the force of the energy from the waves and prevent further erosion of the land.

- **Groynes** – often wooden structures that are placed at along the beach length to prevent the movement of beach material by longshore drift by trapping material on one side.

- **Rock Armour** – large boulders that have been brought in as a barrier to the shoreline to stabilise the cliff by taking the energy from the breaking waves to the cliff edges.

7) Explain 2 different methods of soft engineering and evaluate each one.

- **Beach replenishment** – Adding beach material back on the beach in order to protect the cliffs and the land behind, the material is dredged and moved from other locations. The material is needed to replace what is lost from transportation and erosion.
  Evaluation: Can vary in costs because it is needed regularly, meaning that the cost mounts up. It can negatively impact other areas where the beach material is dredged reducing the beach material there, this can result in the public support being lost.

- **Beach stabilisation** – This involves carving into the cliff face to make it less steep and longer so it slumps less and erodes less easily.

Evaluation: Relatively low cost and is effective at reducing slumping, but it can impact the local communities as it reduces access to the beach.

8) Explain what a shoreline protection method is and their role.
- **Shoreline management plan** – this is when plans are created for management of a length of coast, including the natural processes, human and environmental needs.
- **There are 4 different methods:**

Hold the line: Allow natural processes to shape the coastline

Advance the line: Maintain the existing coast by building defences

Managed realignment: Build new defences outwards into the sea

No intervention: Allow land to flood, construct new line of defence inland

- The SMP will evaluate the area and will look at factors before deciding the right solution for the coastline. It will consider the land is of low value, risk to people and businesses. Hold the line and no intervention are very inexpensive in the short term although if land erodes there may be a need to compensate people for the loss of businesses, land and homes.

9) Explain how seasonal weather effects the coastline.
Stormy weather that brings unseasonal high tides and windy weather called storm surge. These can have a significant impact on the coastline, especially areas of fragile coastline. Recent storms in the last 5 years have resulted in serious disruption including 2014 when a section of the sea wall in Dawlish, Devon, collapsed and left the railway to Cornwall.

10) Assess using an example how coastal landscapes and communities are affected by climate change.
Rising sea levels – with the increasing rate of sea levels areas that were already vulnerable experience further flooding and this increases the impact on people. Costs of protecting the coastline are considerable and therefore difficult for some countries to afford it.
Consider which case study you will use – Small Island Developing States (SIDS) such as Maldives is a good one as there is impact on crops and tourism well documented, long term impacts and its link to development.

KEY IDEA: 2.2 Shaping the landscape – rivers and river management

1. Name two features in each of the river course.

Upper

v-shape valley

Interlocking spurs

Middle

meander

Oxbow lake

Lower

Floodplains

delta

2. Explain how a waterfall is formed with use of a series of diagrams.

Don't get caught out by drawing one!!

This is a simple diagram that you can draw very quickly in the exam – make sure your explanations are developed appropriately.

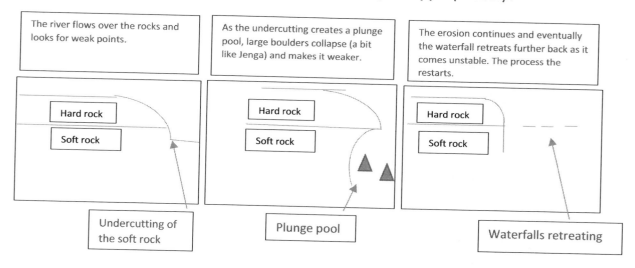

The river flows over the rocks and looks for weak points.

As the undercutting creates a plunge pool, large boulders collapse (a bit like Jenga) and makes it weaker.

The erosion continues and eventually the waterfall retreats further back as it comes unstable. The process the restarts.

Hard rock

Soft rock

Hard rock

Soft rock

Hard rock

Soft rock

Undercutting of the soft rock

Plunge pool

Waterfalls retreating

3. Draw and annotate a diagram of a river / drainage basin.

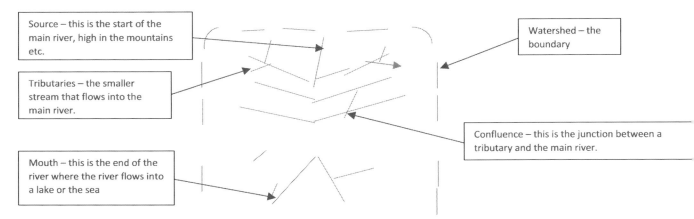

Source – this is the start of the main river, high in the mountains etc.

Tributaries – the smaller stream that flows into the main river.

Mouth – this is the end of the river where the river flows into a lake or the sea

Watershed – the boundary

Confluence – this is the junction between a tributary and the main river.

4. Name and explain at least two human and two physical causes of flooding.
- **Physical**
    - Steep sides – increase the speed of which water (surface runoff) is moved making flooding more likely.
    - Impermeable rock – this means that water cannot infiltrate into the ground which would reduce the surface runoff, therefore increasing the chance of flooding.

- **Human**
    - Deforestation – by removing the vegetation, the rate of infiltration reduces and the grounds becomes less stable, which increases the risk of flooding.
    - Urbanisation – building on flood plains and the increase use of impermeable surface reduces infiltrations and increases surface runoff.
    -

5. Explain why people have altered a rivers course.
- **Channelization** – straightening the channel in order to build roads, new buildings and reduces flood risk.

6. Explain the causes and impacts of a flash flood that you have studied.

Boscastle 2004

- **Causes**
    - Heavy rainfall on already saturated ground. More than 70mm of rain (the average for the whole of August) fell in just 2 hours - it continued on until 8 inches of rain had fallen.
    - The river had been made narrower due to the building of tourist facilities.

- o The drainage basin has impermeable surfaces and funnel shaped courses as well as having three short rivers that quickly flood.
- **Impacts**
  - o More than 120 people were air lifted to safety by helicopters.
  - o It took 9 months to rebuild, cost £15million and insurance companies had high bills, it could make it difficult to insure in the future.
  - o A new flood defence and a regeneration scheme cost £10 million and were officially opened in October 2008.
  - o

7. Annotate the flood / storm hydrograph below and explain whether it is a flash flood or not and why.

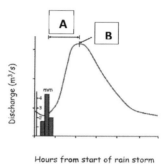

Hours from start of rain storm

A: Lag time – longer time means less likely to be a flash flood.

B: Peak discharge – the highest level of discharge in the river

This storm hydrograph indicates a river that is likely to have a flash flood due to the number of hours it takes for the river to achieve a peak discharge. However, as the falling limb is fairly rapid, depending on the rivers capacity it may not flood on this occasion.

13. Name 3 impacts of flooding and sort these into positive and negative; social and economic consequences and explain each one.

   **Be careful not to pick opposites as often only one will be credited.*

- Loss of farmland (S and E) Negative:

   Revenue and yield will decrease, increasing food prices and putting pressure on farmers' income.

- Deposition of silt (S and E) Positive

   Increase the fertility of the land, leading to increased yields which then increases not only the income from farming but also can lead to higher disposable income which can be used to improve a family's lives.

- Improvement to housing (S) positive

Housing is improved to flood proof the property e.g. electric sockets higher on the wall, tiled flooring which means that the property is more likely to be insurable from future flooding as the cost of repairing is lower.

- Building of flood defences (S and E) N

High costs, some relocation needed of families and businesses, can be unattractive which affects historic areas in particular with tourism.

9. Explain the different methods of river management and how they reduce the risk of flooding.
    - **Embankments:** These are <u>**raised banks**</u> along the river, they effectively make the river deeper so it can hold more water before it floods. Rivers can now increase capacity without causing much damage. Embankments are also built near settlements with wash lands between the embankments and the river.
    - **Flood Barriers:** Flood barriers are either gates or walls that can be permanent or temporary. They're quite expensive and don't look very natural. These can be very effective at stopping flooding. Flood barriers are also used in places where there are a lot of people living.
    - **Straightening and deepening the river:** This is when the **river is made straighter** to make the river flow and channel flow faster so there is less chance of river flooding. It keeps the water levels to a minimum so it is less likely to flood but can use it to make high levels of electricity.

10. Evaluate the effectiveness of different strategies that attempt to reduce the flood risk and evaluate them.

    - *Basic points but you will need to develop these to hit the maximum marks.*
    - **Embankments:** They are very expensive and do not last long (unsustainable). Rivers can now increase capacity without causing much damage.
    - **Flood Barriers:** They're quite expensive and don't look very natural. These can be very effective at stopping flooding.
    - **Environment Agency warnings:** These require investment and technology which restricts the countries that can invest in these. However, people do not always listen to warning systems – they are given on tv, radio and the internet.

KEY IDEA: 2.3 Weather and Climate

1. Describe the distribution of the world climates and name examples.
    - *Distribution – spread – give examples*
    Tundra areas in the extreme northern hemisphere around Greenland, Alaska and the very north of Russia.

Semi-Arid desert – mostly in central to Northern Africa.

2. Describe the weather associated with an anticyclone and depression in both the summer and the winter.
   - **Anticyclone:** settled weather that brings stable weather in the UK.
   - **Summer:** sunshine, very few clouds, dry weather
   - **Winter:** frosty and dry weather
   - **Depression:** weather that we have in the UK more often. The weather is similar in both the summer and winter: brings cloud, rain, wind and generally unsettled weather conditions.

3. Explain the difference between the equatorial and semi-arid climates and explain why this happened.
   - **Semi-arid:** Semi-arid regions receive slightly more rainfall than desert regions - precipitation, of around 25 and 50 cm. Location varies – cold semi-arid are found in temperate zones, likely to occur inland, away from large bodies of water. Hot semi-arid are typically found on the fringe of sub-tropical deserts
   - **Equatorial** – stable climate with very small fluctuations in its annual temperature (24°–28°C), and high precipitation (1,500–5,000 mm a year).
   - **Why:** location - equatorial is along the equator and the semi-arid is further north and south of the equator, narrow band between it and the desert.

4. Explain the global atmospheric circulation model and how it impacts weather in different locations.
   This is moment on a large-scale movement of air, together with circulation of ocean. This is redistributed thermal energy on the surface of the Earth. This movement starts at the equator, the hottest part of the Earth moving warm air. The moment creates winds which moves air from areas of high pressure to areas of low pressure across the planet. As a result, areas experience different levels of rainfall. Low pressure brings high rainfall, high pressure brings low rainfall, as a result it leads to areas of high rainfall, like the tropical rainforests, and areas of dry air, like deserts

5. Using an example, explain how different groups of people were affected by the drought.

   Australia 2003
   - Drought affected farmers as agricultural production was 30% lower than in previous years.
   - Over 70,000 people became unemployed, mainly in wholesale, transport, food production and retailing
   - Homeowners were negatively affected: 170 houses destroyed in Sydney and 4 people killed and 500 houses destroyed in Canberra

6. Explain why the UK has a mild, wet climate.

- UK is a small island and is affected by the ocean. It is strongly influenced by the **MARITIME** because of the air masses and ocean currents crossing the Atlantic Ocean. We have 5 clear distinct seasons and our weather is variable throughout the year.
- The following the main factors that affect the UK's climate are:
    - Latitude
    - Jet stream and its effect on movement of air masses.
    - Effect of ocean currents
    - Altitude and Aspect

7. Describe the links between the distribution of climates and the distribution of ecosystems.
    - The climate of each area affects the uniqueness of ecosystem development. These factors include: *number of daylight hours, wind, precipitation, temperature.*
    - Distribution – areas with high daylight hours, temperatures and rainfall – sees the greatest ecosystems however are fragile to changes and therefore with any climate change, the ecosystem changes quickly (rainfall decreasing leads to semi-arid or even desert).

8. Explain the consequences of extreme weather events.
    ** focus on the term *consequences* **
    e.g. People in some areas unable to get insurance due to the frequent flooding.
    Environmental impacts – including land becoming contaminated by flood water.

9. Using the extreme weather event that you have studied, give 3 causes of the event and 3 impact.

    Storm Desmond 2005 – widespread storm

    - **Causes:**
        - Rainfall in this storm broke all previous UK records including Honister in Cumbria received 341.4mm (13.4in) of rain.
        - Increased building on floodplain including around Cockermouth.
        - Heavy rain fell on land that had already been saturated in Cumbria.

    - **Impact:**
        - Homeless: temporary accommodation costs - the government helped by providing local authorities with over £500 for each household affected.
        - Over 60,000 homes without power.
        - One person died in Cumbria and about 40 schools closed in Cumbria.

10. Using the extreme weather event that you have studied, assess how the event impacted the people and environment.
    ** *Assess* – focus on the damage and impact caused and NOT the causes!!!

You could use Storm Desmond case study.

Some of the impacts on the environment:

- Rivers were significantly altered with increased rates of erosion.
- Landslides and mudslides were reported e.g. on the A83 at Rest and Be Thankful
- Soil contamination

Some of the impacts on people:

- Over 60,000 homes without power this means families forced to evacuate, unable to live in their homes, unsafe to cook etc.
- Rail services disrupted which means people experienced delays or cancellations which impacts on being able to get to work etc.
- Cost over £760 million in insurance claims. Some homes at risk of not being able to get insurance or certainly not affordable insurance.

KEY IDEA: 2.4: Climate change - cause and effect

1. **Describe how climate has changed to include glacial and inter-glacial periods.**
   - High rates of fluctuation – particularly in the last 400000.
   - Inter-glacial – polar ice has retreated.
   - Glacial – polar ice has reached further south, covering large parts of the earth.

2. **Name one greenhouse gas.**
   Carbon dioxide, methane, water vapour

3. **Describe the processes that create the greenhouse effect.**
   Think of it in stages – sun rays come into the atmosphere, only a small amount of short-wave radiation is absorbed, some are reflected out. The solar energy heats up the surface of the earth which sends long wave heat energy into the atmosphere, however some can't escape and get absorbed by the greenhouse gases. This means that the heat waves (longwave) remains and this results in the earth warming up (almost like it boosting up).

4. **Explain how the increased meat consumption has impacted greenhouse gases.**
   Number of factors – increased in global population, increase in income = eating meat is seen as a sign of affluence together with increase in ready meals. As a result, the number of cattle being reared has increased dramatically especially in South America.

5. Explain one other human activity as **one** contributory factor in global warming.

   Rice production, car ownership, air travel. Focus on why there has been an increase and quote figures to support.

6. Describe how climate change affects tourism in one region you have studied.

   Case study – Bahamas

   Tourism is a big economic contributor to the region – over 40% GDP revenue. It is one of the SIDS (Small Island Developing states) – and is vulnerable to climate change – including sea level rises including flooding and loss of beaches, farmland contaminated, infrastructure damaged.

7. Describe the global initiatives to reduce the impact of climate change.

   Number of different initiatives that are agreements and don't necessary become law – think Trump and the Paris agreement!!!

   Paris Agreement – 2015

   Different rates of emissions depending on countries level of development.

8. Describe the initiatives that have already taken place in the UK.
   - National level – government set targets on recycling
   - Changing energy resources in the UK – movement towards fracking as an example.

   Investment in renewable technologies.

9. Explain the role that individuals and government in the UK can play in reducing the risk of climate change.
   - Individual – finding ways to increase recycling, reducing carbon emissions from transport (increase use of public transport use).
   - Government – use incentives to encourage businesses and individuals to switching to more energy efficient methods. Investment in transport improvements e.g. HS2 to encourage public transport use.

10. Assess the way climate change affects water supply in one region.

   Africa – but name regions!

   More irregular patterns of rainfall, including North African region. Water stress – not enough access to water. Increased mosquitoes – especially in East Africa, in high dense areas of Kenya and Ethiopia.

THEME 3: ENVIRONMENTAL CHALLENGES

KEY IDEA: 3.1: How ecosystems function and 3.2 Ecosystems under threat

1. Describe the location of two contrasting ecosystems.
   - Biomes – large scale ecosystem
   - Tundra – extreme north region around Russia, Greenland and Alaska
   - Tropical Rainforest – around the central belt of the equator, in Brazil, Australia, and central Africa e.g. DR Congo

2. Explain why energy or water resource production can have negative impacts on the environment.

   Building of dams – used to regulate water supply and can be used as Hydro Electric Power. Impacts – deposition of silt within the reservoir and up stream of the dam, causing changes of the PH level of the water for example impacting on the animals / flora and fauna. Energy – dams HEP the noise can disrupt wildlife. Oil exploitation – risk of spillage, contamination of the land including water.

3. Demonstrate how poor land management has affected one region of hot semi-arid grassland.
   Farming – over grazing on fragile land due to low income, population growth, war (restricts access to other income etc), soil moisture very fragile to change, irregular and low precipitation.

4. What are 'buttress roots' and why are they necessary?
   One adaptation of plants in rainforests, roots that are formed on the surface due to the shallow soil and the height and weight of the trees.

5. Define the following terms:
   a. Consumer: Organisms that eat producers (e.g. caterpillar)
   b. Tertiary: Animal that eats primary and / or secondary consumers for energy
   c. Biotic: Living or once-living elements of an ecosystem

6. Trees in tropical rainforests have adapted to their biome. What does adaptation mean?
   Adaption is the processes whereby the trees (and other plants and animals) change (adapt) their features to the climate and vegetation surrounding them. These including buttress roots, trip tip leaves etc.

7. What are the impacts of human exploitation of your chosen ecosystem? Consider environmental, social and economic.

   Tropical Rainforest – watch Bruce Parry Amazon if you've not got a case study from school.

- **Environmental** – oil spillage, water contamination, deforestation
- **Social** – indigenous tribes losing their land, indigenous communities under threat from new diseases from outsides
- **Economic** – deforestation bringing income into the communities (attracts the young men especially from the indigenous communities to move etc), mining and cattle ranching is big income earners for the wealthy who have "invested" in the areas (often illegally without land rights).

8. Looking at your case study, evaluate the outcomes of local scale conservation strategies.
   - Evaluate – look at the positive and negative
   - Depending on your case study:
   - you must look at what makes it successful or unsuccessful who have won and lost – communities impact on preventing further loss of environment wide spread impacts
   - There are lots of case studies online – search GCSE geography conservation

9. Describe and explain the main threats to the hot semi-arid grassland.
   - **Overgrazing** - increasing in grazing cattle on the land taking away the vegetation. (E) This can lead to desertification as the soil is fragile meaning it risks fires, further desertification and livestock struggling to be fed – impacting on the local communities.
   - **Wildfires** – fires that start in grasslands, spreading quickly (E) due to the dry land, lack of water, risks lives.
   - **Tourism** – visitors coming from richer countries to view animals (and landscapes). (E) Increased accommodations being built (even temporary), increased car emissions with higher numbers, multiplier effect with increased in people moving into the area and facilities opening (e.g. Golf courses).
   - **Climate change** – changes in precipitation rates for example. (E) increased risks of wildfires and crop yields decreasing.
   - **Deforestation** – clearing the land for firewood and land for grazing. (E) Due to the population growth and demand for land, forests are cleared, exposing the soil increasing soil erosion and then increasing the chance of desertification and wildfires.

10. Assess the sustainable management strategies are necessary in hot semi-arid grasslands.
    - Depending on your case study but focus on: MANAGEMENT – methods to stop further decline in the environment but still also the local communities to earn income.
    - Strategies to reduce overgrazing such as encouraging people to farm using traditional methods of fertilising, drip irrigation (to stop wasting water and prevent soil erosion), planning trees (schemes to reimburse communities in some areas), preventing poaching by encouraging the community to

take an active role in protecting the wildlife (e.g. Masai have been successful in this).
- Lots of case studies online.

KEY IDEA 3.2 Water Resources and Management

1. Define the following terms:
    a. water footprint: The amount of water needed to produce an item e.g. food, clothing.
    b. water storage: Where water is kept in a large amount e.g. lake

2. Explain the changing demands for water in the last 100 years,
    Demand has increased – population increase (food production and personal use) and industrialisation (including production of goods and cars). Water demands first increased in the established developed countries such as UK, USA and Germany who mostly have a stable water supply however this has now spread across the world into areas with more vulnerable water supply.

3. Explain the link between population change and economic growth.
    Higher population means there is a demand for more water – food, clothing, employment. This has led to pressure on water within the whole world. Secondary industries e.g. factories producing products like clothing, use high amounts of water, countries are normally very keen for economic development so there is often very few regulations to prevent over use of water.

4. Describe the concept of over-abstraction and the impact this has on areas.
    - Definition – over-abstraction is the removal of water from storage, quicker than it can be recharged.
    - Impacts – further pressure on water, often in areas with indigenous communities who use water in traditional ways (e.g. farming) which impacts on their lives (e.g. poverty) as well as increasing the risk of desertification. Impact on ecosystems such as wetlands, soils at risk of salinization and risk of diseases (both human and animals) spreading.

5. Explain the need for a water transfer scheme.
    Water transfer – moving water from one area to another. It is normally used to support developments such as factories, HEP and farming needs in order to support the population of the area. The demand for water and supply might cause water stress due to the deficit in the amount.

6. Studying your case study, explain the needs for the water transfer scheme and the impact on the environment and the people.
    - Various Case Studies out there – Colorado River (USA – Mexico), Lesotho Highlands Water Project or the Tigris-Euphrates River.

- Conflict – who owns the water?? Who has rights?? Pressure on water has led to a number of significant issues.
- Impact on people – consider the farmers, those who need relocating, historic land that is flooded.
- Impact on environment - once the river has management upstream, people lower down in the river course lose water and also management reduces flooding (positive for most but farmer often rely on flooding to bring slit to support fertilise the land).

KEY IDEA 3.3: Desertification

1. Define the following terms:
    a. hot desert: An area with less than 250 mm of rainfall a year, has two district seasons which vary with temperatures from **summer**, when the temperature ranges between 35-40°C, and **winter**, when the temperature ranges between 20-30°C.

    b. over-grazing: Grazing of livestock (farm animals) which has a negative impact on the soil and vegetation.

2. Explain how desertification is related to the global circulation of the atmosphere and the dominance of high-pressure systems.
    Unpredictable patterns of precipitation are the leading cause of desertification – areas do not have a set rainfall. Locations such as the Sahel has long dry seasons for over 9 months and 3 months of rainfall. The seasonal patterns are very fragile – the short wet season coincides with the movement of the ITCZ – this pattern is not a fixed which can lead to shorter wet seasons. This pattern can lead to run off of land, removing the soil (making it more vulnerable) and also the reducing the amount of water that reaches the aquifers which need to be restocked.

3. Explain how changing patterns of vegetation can lead to desertification.
    Poor farming methods whereby natural vegetation is cleared for the growth of commercial vegetation can put more pressure on fragile land. The fallow period (traditionally land is abandoned for between 8-15 years on average) is often ignored and reduced to only 2-3 year which means the land is even more vulnerable – leading to the soil becoming exposed to erosion of both wind and rainfall.

4. Explain how economic development has increased desertification.
    Introduction of commercial farming methods (also known as agri-businesses) which is where land has been leased (or bought) by large businesses for farming. This has happened in many African countries. Single crops were planted to make quick profit and the demand has increased, leading to more commercial farming. The land is now allowed to fallow for the necessary time

which over time increases the risk of desertification. Bio-fuels are often grown due to the demand.

14. Explain at least two strategies used with local communities to manage the problems of desertification.
    Strategies:
    - Tree planning scheme – help with infiltration of rainwater, supports soil stability and prevents further erosion, supports nutrients within the foil bringing back fertility.

    - Rain Water harvesting investment – using techniques like bund, collecting from roofs to help infiltration, etc

    - These are low cost, easy to maintain which allows local communities to continue to use after the NGOs have left.

5. Explain two international strategies and the impact on desertification.
    Further development of NGO with government funding and loans from international organisation. These are often large-scale strategies like in Q5. For example, Great Green Wall of Africa case study.
    NGO: non-governmental organisations such as Water Aid, Oxfam etc

Fieldwork booklet answers

- The answers in this booklet are suggestions that you could develop further. Each board has a slightly different way in allocating marks. It is important that you know your fieldworks in detail – you will be examined on both!!!

Geographical and Numeracy Skills Answers

1. Here is the temperature of one location over 45 years. Use this data to answer the questions:

    a. What is the range of this data?
       8°C (lowest 0 to the highest +8)
    b. Calculate the mean.
       2.1 (add all the data up and divide by the number of data sets).
    c. Suggest the trends of the temperature at this location.
       Temperature has low fluctuating with a small range with one anomaly in 1975.

1970	1975	1980	1985	1990	1995	2000	2005	2010	2015
3 °C	8 °C	3 °C	2 °C	1 °C	0 °C	0 °C	1 °C	1 °C	2 °C

2. Complete the pie chart below with the missing data and key:

In B&B/ Hotel	Camping	Staying with friends/ family	Other
30	0	5	15

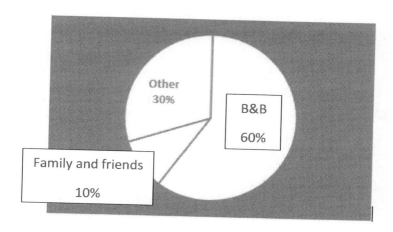

3. The results of the river fieldwork looking at the size of pebbles is shown in the table below.

Sample	Pebble size in centimetres
1	15
2	8
3	7
4	9
5	11
6	4
7	12
8	10
9	6
10	12
11	21

a. What is the range of the data? 17

b. Calculate the interquartile range of the pebble size data. Show your working in the space below.

Order the data – watch for duplicate numbers and check the number of data sets match!!

4 6 7 8 9 10 11 12 12 15 21

- The **median** is the (11 + 1)/2 = 6th value.   **10**
- The **lower quartile** is the (11 + 1)/4 = 3rd value.   **7**
- The **upper quartile** is the 3(11 + 1)/4 th = 9th value.   **12**

   c. Suggest how you could display this information and justify your reasons.

Bar graph or line to show the data – the sites are clear and the trend is shown. Develop your justification – consider how patterns / trends support the theory studied, help identify sites etc.

4. Using the grid below, give the 4 figure and 6 figures.

- 4 Figure
     a. £ - 1443
     b. $ - 1141
     c. ? – 1342
     d. @ - 1243
     e. # - 1340
     f. & - 1140

- 6 Figure
     a. £ - 147433
     b. $ - 112419
     c. ? – 136421
     d. @ - 123438
     e. # - 134409
     f. & - 117403

Your Human fieldwork

There are number of different methods and techniques, the answers here are suggestions – the examiner will not know exactly what you did.

Questions

1. Explain which primary method was the most successful in collecting enough data.
    Look at the different methods and which gave you the most data.
    Traffic count – 2 x 20 min, at 15 sites. This was successful as you could see areas of hot spots, see the flow clearly, identify areas of congestion.

2. Explain which method was the most difficult to collect.
   For example, questionnaire
   Limitation = too much data, if questions are not well-constructed questions / open / too many options then difficult to analysis.

3. Describe one method in detail, step by step.
   Pedestrian count:
   a. Prep - identified on a map 15 sites, worked in pairs, checked watches to ensure starting at the same time.
   b. Counted for 20 min at 10.50 and 2.20
   c. counted right and left = recorded as a tally
   d. at the end = tallied

4. Suggest how you could improve the methods used.
   Added an additional time around lunch time to compare the lunchtime flow.
   Conduct an environmental quality survey / bi polar survey to see if the areas are impacted at the time.

5. Explain the HUMAN aspect that you focused on.
   This will depend on what you studied but could be increased visitor numbers / increased urbanisation / increased retail / increased sport.

6. Using your data presentation methods, assess the results show and link it to your aim.
   Pedestrian count – isopleth map to show the results.
   Able to identify the flow / hot spots of pedestrian. (LINK TO AIM)
   The darker shaded the higher data.

7. Evaluate the reliability of your data presentation.
   Isopleth map
   Strengths – easy to see areas of high results – hot spots
   Weakness – not clear to see individual sites results due to the range, difficult to overlay AM and PM data.

8. Suggest one other data presentation method that could have been used and explain why.
   Pie Charts of questionnaire data
   Using excel or similar to display the results – clear to display, easy to analysis and able to analysis with other data (e.g. images) and cross reference.

9. Summaries the main findings of your fieldwork.

Consider the main points and how it links to the purpose of your fieldwork. Use a few brief evidences e.g. data at 3 points to support your points.

10. Evaluate the usefulness of your fieldwork.
Consider if it helped you gather enough data to answer the aim, what worked well, why, what could you improved on and why. Don't forget to look at data collection and presentation.

Your Physical fieldwork

1. Suggest two reasons why undertaking a risk assessment is vital for planning a fieldwork.
To ensure the location and activities are suitable. Lots of things have to be considered such as weather / time, too close to river, safety of tide times etc.

2. Assess suitability of your location.
You need to consider the risk assessment and also can you collect enough data to answer your fieldwork. Consider access, ability to collect enough data etc.

3. Describe how you collected one secondary method.
Historic photographs – use library / internet to collect, can overlap with OS Map to track changes.

4. Explain which secondary method was the least successful.
Visitor numbers in the past using research / sources as it has too many variables such as weather / collection methods / locations (trip advisors reviews).

5. Explain which primary method was the most difficult to collect.
Groyne height – difficult to access all the groyne, difficult to get accurate measurements due to tide times.

6. Suggest how you could improve one method used.
Groyne height – measure at the same point - top middle and bottom – only go at low tide. Take samples such sediment to develop the results.

7. Explain what PHYSICAL aspect that you focused on.
Impact of longshore drift on the coastline - How and why the rates of coastal recession vary along a stretch of coast.

8. Using one data presentation, evaluate the reliability of your data.
Groyne height graphs – do each graph separately then put on a map next to each groyne – easy to annotate and show the changes.

9. Summaries the main findings of your fieldwork.
    Consider what the main findings were – include some key facts and results. Need to be specific e.g. the pattern that Longshore drift except groyne 12 but that could be due to the poor state of repair of the groin.

10. Evaluate the usefulness of your fieldwork.
    You'll need to be specific to your fieldwork but consider these:
    a. Think did it answer your aims?
    b. What worked best?
    c. What could you improve on?

Unseen fieldwork example 1

1. Suggest the usefulness of geographical theory (background) in planning your fieldwork.
    Think about the links between your fieldwork and theory you've been taught e.g. bradshaw model for rivers, the process of longshire drift. Make sure you are clear about this with your work.

2. Explain the purpose of setting aims / hypothesis.
    Make sure you understand what your aims / hypothesis are set out to find – you need to be specific. The exam might ask you to link it to another question.

3. Identify whether these are primary or secondary methods of data collection and the write a brief description of how you would collect the data.

	Primary	Secondary	Describe how you would collect data using this method
Transect	X		Along one road, at every interval (20m foe example) take photographs and complete a survey / observations.
GIS		X	Use GIS program to collect data information such as mapping population.
Pedestrian count	X		At least 10 sites, measuring in pairs simultaneously for 20 minutes, using a tally chart to record / look at direction travelled. Possibly do more than once in order to look at the increase etc
Traffic count	X		
Maps e.g. Bing, OS		X	Using the software program, search the location, adapt to the scale needed, then screenshot to be able to put into text. Can identify areas to research, identify places what are changing / vulnerable, support risk assessment and planning.

Bi-polar or Environmental Quality Survey	X		Identify at least 4 sites (ideally 6 or more). Using set statements (e.g. lots of litter to no litter) and give a score (-3 to +3). Add all the scores together to give a total.
Groyne height method	X		Measure the sediment on both sides of the groin, tape measure and record it.
Historical data		X	Research using library or internet search engines.

4. What does the phrase "data presentation" mean?
   This is how the data results are shown – you need to be clear about the methods used if required to.
5. What is the difference between a closed question and an open questionnaire? Suggest a reason why one would be the most useful type to use. Open – like asking for comments, not giving options for answers.
   Closed – multiple choices – easier to look at patterns and work out stats.
6. Using the data below, decide which data presentation is the most suitable and explain why.

How did you travel here today?

Bus / Coach	4
Car	30
Walk	4
Motorbike	20
Other	0

Bar graph = shows the other category which had no data – pie chart wouldn't show this option.

7. Using the photographs below, answer the questions:

a) Name the method: proportionate arrows

Suggest what data would be suitable to use this method.

Traffic count – can split into vehicle types within the arrow as done here.

Describe the method used.

Create a key (e.g. 1mm = 2 vehicles) for the width, the length remains the same for each site.

Explain the reasons for using this method.

Shows the flow, direction and vehicle type. Can be useful to show hotspots.

Suggest an alternative method of presenting this data. Isopleth or mini graph per site.

b) Name the method: trip line

Suggest what data would be suitable to use this method.

Show locations travelled to or from a place.

Describe the method used.

Each line represents one person, drawn from their point of origin to the location.

Explain the reasons for using this method.

Very easy to display the information, makes it clear the areas where people mainly travelled from, easier to show how large its sphere of influence is.

Suggest an alternative method of presenting this data. Bar graph

8. Give one advantage and one disadvantage of this method:
   ADV: Clear to show the results of opinions especially and percentages.
   DIS: those with small results or none at all are difficult to analysis

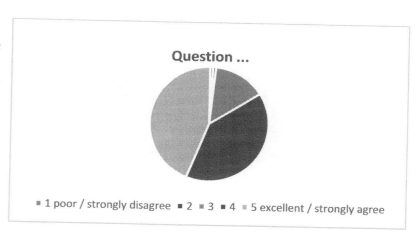

9. Analysis the following graph below, based different fieldworks.

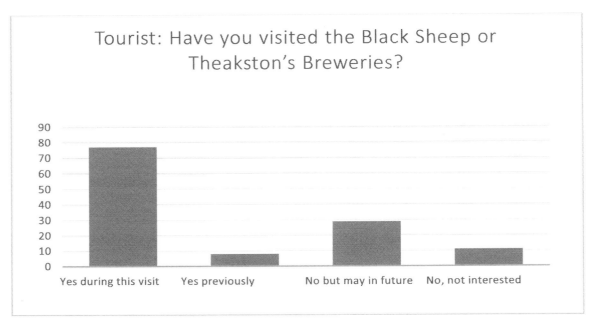

You need to quote data e.g. 77 people answered yes during this visit THEN SAY WHAT IT MEANS it has a large number of visitors, compared to the "no not interested" which has 10, suggesting that most people are coming to the area for the breweries, this shows the breweries are big draw to the area.

10. Explain the differences between qualitative and quantitative data. Use at least on example for each.
    Qualitative – these are statements or things that you can develop. Consider bipolar / environmental quality survey– where you score a place etc.
    Quantitative data – this is data that you collected e.g. height of groynes

11. What was the method that you used to collect / conduct a flow?
    Counts – traffic / pedestrian
    a. What were the limitations of this method?
    Limited to one or two periods of time. Limited locations
    b. Suggest **two** ways that you could make your use of flow more reliable.
    Conducts two counts – AM and PM for example or 10am and lunch depending on your hypothesis.
    Could look at different days to compare flows or time of year.
    Consider expanding the points to develop these.

12. Suggest how you could investigate sustainability within a physical environment.
    Coastal or rivers – look at the vulnerability and management from flood risk.
    Method – GIS map, Environment Quality Survey, photographs, Questionnaire
    Data Presentation – mapping, annotate images, graphing of EQS

Specific topic fieldwork questions

Coastal

1. Explain how the rate of coastal erosion can be measured using secondary data.

    Depending on your method: GIS mapping – look at the rate of erosion within a time frame.

    Historic data e.g. villages that have been lost and when? Overlay on map,

2. Explain why house prices are likely to be higher in areas with multiple coastal defences.

    Consider the factors – if houses are less likely to be lost due to protection then they will command a higher price as they will survive coastal erosion. They are likely to be able to get a mortgage compared to an area without protection as those will either be cash only or under compulsory purchase orders.

3. Describe how you could create an investigating to whether the sea defences appear to be adequate / well maintained at a location (e.g. Hornsea).

    You will need to look at the area and create aim e.g. "The sea defences at Hornsea are essential to prevent erosion of the coastline and maintain the beach as a tourist facility."

    Research the protection methods, research the past erosion, look at the rate of erosion. Transect of the area to look at the different methods and impact on the areas. Data presentation – map with photographs to show each site on transect (likely to show that further from the coastline that housing becomes bigger / more developed / grander etc).

4. Suggest which data collection methods you would use. Explain your reasons why.

    Methodology – two transects – one in an area with protection and one without. Take photographs to record, EQS / bipolar, questionnaires. These could show the contrast between the areas – it could be supported with other data to be evaluated.

River

1. Describe how you would investigate the vulnerability of a town from flooding.

    Mapping tools e.g. environment agency to identify areas with past flooding. Further secondary research looking at house prices in two areas, questionnaire to see what local people say.

2. Suggest how you would investigate the success of river defences.

Bipolar / EQS – look at the types of methods.

Track house prices (e.g. right move website) – to see if they have increased more than the average and to see if there are areas that have decreased.

Photographical evidence

Transect between areas.

3. Describe how you would investigate to see if the Bradshaw model (or other geographical theory) applied to a river.

   Investigate a river that you can see all courses of a river. At each stage conduce the following – bedload, channel width, channel depth, velocity. Look for evidence of human management.

4. Evaluate the usefulness of the environment agencies flood map planning and / or other GIS within planning of a fieldwork.

   Create a list of positive points for the techniques – overlay multiple data which builds a depth of location, able to conduct historic and future, highly accurate, can be used for physical geography such as a river course with vegetation and gradient.

Urban environment

1. Describe how you would investigate to see what the land use pattern of your chosen location.

   Transect across from the CBD to the outer suburbs. You could take photographic evidence, Environmental Quality Survey / BiPolar, questionnaire, house price.

2. Discuss how you can use secondary data to display data (e.g. CCTV)

   Depending on the data you could do a word oddle to display key words. You could map the sites of CCTV and code to show the number of times the footage was used for calls to police. Or plot the number of cameras in an area – show the higher numbers vs low.

3. Suggest how you would investigate the change of demographic in an urban area.

   Census details – show the changing nature – can display as bar graph of the change in the main groups.

   Investigate change of facilities in the area such as school, youth clubs, retirement groups = use questionnaires, research new buildings (housing for families or over 50s), facilities closing.

4. Evaluate the usefulness of the census as secondary data.

Census – every 10 years, categories very broad, areas change, questions not consistent every year. Very useful as a starting point for an investigation.

Rural environment

1. Discuss how pedestrian counts at different times can be useful in showing the impact of tourism.

High numbers at lunch time suggest visitors are in the area = identify areas of interest, identify transport e.g. parking. Can do multiple visits AM / PM / MIDDAY

2. Suggest which methods of data collection would be useful in investigating the impact of tourism.

Traffic count – repeat at the same points as pedestrian counts. Car park study – look at number of cars / coaches / look at the time on parking tickets (all day compared to one hour).

3. Discuss the limitation of 2 methods of data collection.

Questionnaire: closed questions limited the answer, have to get people to answer and rely on them being truthful. Difficult to gather and analysis results.

Car park = weather depending results, car park might not have enough spaces so not enough data (would have to look at parking issues such as double parking)

4. Evaluate the usefulness of secondary sources such as trip advisor.

Gives you dates and locations of the reviewer – so you get to see the sphere of influence. You can see the number of tourist facilities in the area and whether local people use the facilities.

Unseen Fieldwork Example

Part 1:

1. Create a hypothesis or aim to investigate the area and the issues seen in the photographs.

Due to the large number of visitors to Grassington, the footpath along the river Wharfe will have suffered from erosion and therefore will need to be managed.

2. Explain the advantages of the location shown above for creating a fieldwork enquiry.

    Honeypot site, high visitor numbers, protected area.

3. Describe 2 primary data collection methods that would be appropriate to gather information on your hypothesis. Explain your reasons why.

    Footpath erosion measurements – to see areas of visitor numbers, able to see the contrast between management and no management.
    Photographs – to record the sites to support annotation.
    Visitor numbers – counting number of people walking on the path.

4. Suggest a secondary data collection method that would support your aim.

    Research visitor facilities or management in the local area e.g. national trust produces results.

5. Identify 2 possible hazards and create a risk assessment based on this.

    River – flooding, bank unstable, accidently fall in.

    Footpath – trip or fall on the tree roots, difficult in access if need emergency services needed.

6. Suggest the possible reasons for footpath management as seen in photograph E.

    High visitor numbers to protect and prevent further erosion. National Trust or similar bodies could have funded or raise money to stop further management.

7. Using graph below, evaluate the usefulness of the data presentation seen.

    Shows each sites clearly. Footpath erosion above 1.5m (national trust recommended width) – green below, red above. Site 4 is clearly very wide with the 5m above the 1.5m. To improve you could add photographs to each graph to show the issues.

8. Returning in 12 months is one possible method of gathering further data. Suggest advantages and disadvantages to this.

    ADV: can track further erosion or show if the management is being successful (e.g. no secondary paths forming).

    DIS sites might not be easy to identify exactly the same. If weather is different on the dates it could reflect the width and make it more difficult to identify where the path starts.

Part 2:

9. Using the images, identify 2 issues that could be occurring in the town.
   Congestion – pedestrian or traffic (double yellow lines), lack of outdoor space e.g. pavements congested with furniture making it difficult to walk past.

10. Suggest 2 methods of collecting data that students could take part to look to look at the number of visitors in the area. Explain your choices.
    Pedestrian Count: able to identify areas with high levels of pedestrian.
    Environmental Quality Survey / Bipolar count: Record at 6 sites – look at a set level of statements and score them – easy to look at areas where there are potential issues.
    Noise level – can use an app to record the noise at sites looking at from cars.

11. Suggest the three groups of people that might be targeted for a questionnaire. Explain the reasons why.
    Shopkeepers – see if they are aimed at tourists, look at issues they have regarding tourism.
    Local people – see if they are having issues such as difficulty in

12. Complete the bi-polar / Environmental Quality Survey.

	5	4	3	2	1	
Attractive location						Unattractive location
No Litter						Lots of litter
Few pedestrians						Overcrowded
No street furniture						Lots of street furniture
Wide road						Narrow road

13. Using the example below of presenting the EQS / Bipolar results, suggest the limitations of this method. (*HINT*: use of a 0 axis and a negative score)

   0 suggests neutral which isn't useful

   The minus can be too negative – therefore the model in Q12 is more useful.

   Too many categories to make it difficult to read.

14. Students have attempted to write up the results from their study. Studying the two examples, annotate with positive (P) and areas to improve (AI) on in their write up:

A	Site 1 was near the centre of Grassington. It scored low (-2 and -3) for traffic and lots of street furniture (p) but that was to be expected (AI). There was some greenery and this was scored at +1 as a result. The overall result for this site was -6 and the environment is clearly affected by tourism. (p)
B	Using the EQS results I noticed that sites that scored better (+1-+3) were further from the town centre (P). These had higher scores on little traffic and greenery. However, they often had less few locations with street furniture (AI) (unlike site 1 and 3 which was -3) however these were clearly more residential than site 1 and 3 which were in the town and more tourist areas (P).

Look at the explanation and link to the data. Needs to be specific to the question, link it back and using EQA / Bipolar a total score is useful to give an overview.

15. Evaluate the proposed fieldwork and whether it will achieve its aims.

Looking at the two locations gives a broad study, lots of data collection methods to be researched, some might be affected by the weather if poor or unusually very good as it can give numbers too high / low. Useful to return but footpath data difficult to repeat at same points.

Appendix

Revision Timetable

Week Commencing _____

Monday	
Time	**Revision Subject/Topics**
	Homework
5-minute break	
5-minute break	
5-minute break	

Tuesday	
Time	**Revision Subject/Topics**
	Homework
5-minute break	
5-minute break	
5-minute break	

Wednesday	
Time	**Revision Subject/Topics**
	Homework
5-minute break	
5-minute break	
5-minute break	

Thursday	
Time	**Revision Subject/Topics**
	Homework
5-minute break	
5-minute break	
5-minute break	

Friday	
Time	**Revision Subject/Topics**
	Homework
5-minute break	
5-minute break	
5-minute break	

Saturday	
Time	**Revision Subject/Topics**
	Homework
5-minute break	
5-minute break	
5-minute break	
5-minute break	
5-minute break	
5-minute break	

Sunday	
Time	**Revision Subject/Topics**
	Homework
5-minute break	
5-minute break	
5-minute break	
5-minute break	
5-minute break	
5-minute break	

Revision Planner

Subject	Group	Priority	Number of hours per week

Recommended:	Groups:	Priority:
	Core	High (+2 hours)
	A-level choice	Medium (+1 hour)
	Subjects I struggle	Medium (+1 hour)
	Subjects I comfortable with	Low (1 hour)

Revision Tracker

Subject	Planned hours per week	Actual hours revised per week													
Week commencing															